from WILLIAMSBURG KITCHENS

Compiled by
CAROLYN GAERTNER

Illustrated by
HARRIETTE BARKER

ISBN: 0-9638258-0-1

Library of Congress Catalog Card Number: 68-21709

All Rights Reserved

© Bicast Publishing Co.

1993

Cover Photo By: Fred Miller

The Publishers wish to thank Kevin Tabaac and Taliaferro's Kitchen for the use of their facilities to create the cover picture.

Bicast Publishing Co.

Box 2676
Williamsburg, Virginia 23187

Abbreviations

tsp. ....teaspoon
tbsp. ....tablespoon
cup ....cup
pt. ....pint
qt. ....quart
oz. ....ounce
lb. ....pound

Food Measures

3 tsps. ....1 tablespoon
2 tbsps. ....1 fluid ounce
4 tbsps. ....¼ cup
6 tbsps. ....⅜ cup
8 tbsps. ....½ cup
16 tbsps. ....1 cup
1 cup ....8 fluid ounces
2 cups ....1 pint
2 pts. ....1 quart

Oven Temperatures

Very slow ....250°F and 275°F
Slow ....300°F and 325°F
Moderate ....350°F and 375°F
Hot ....400°F and 425°F
Very hot ....450°F and 475°F
Extremely hot....500°F and 525°F

Order Blanks for Additional Books on Page 155

CONTENTS

FOREWORD

Turn your tastebuds back to the gracious days of Colonial Virginia. Picture the cheerful atmosphere of a plantation kitchen with its homey fireplace, hanging utensils and sparkling copper pots. Relax and let your tensions drift away in the rich aroma of prized old Southern dishes. Old recipes, passed along the generations and added to with meticulous, loving preparation, are keynotes of Southern hospitality. Virginians, along the York and James and in Williamsburg, were grateful for their bountiful gardens, fields, orchards and waterways. They were proud of their culinary art. Cooking wasn't a task . . . it was a joyful pleasure.

Recipes brought from England were enriched with cooking methods and dishes learned from the Indians. This gourmet blend became famed far and wide as "Virginia Cookin'". Early Colonial imagination ran wild with Indian corn meal, creating hundreds of delightful, mouth-watering corn bread recipes. If you want to see eyes sparkle with new lustre, mention to the man who has partaken of them . . . flaky biscuits, light golden muffins, airy popovers, tender griddlecakes and crusty, brown Sally Lund bread! Each of these is truly "a meal in itself."

Summer gardens poured forth a cornucopia of crisp vegetables. Early crops were preserved for winter use. Corn, apples, green beans were dried; cucumbers and beans were pickled and apples, potatoes and cabbage were stored in underground cellars. In preparing these, wonderful flavoring secrets were explored; each cook sought to out-do the others and . . . regardless of season . . . vegetables were a festive delight!

The Indians gave us "homely" hominy. Colonial cooks gave it a variety and spice that made it a tradition. They vied with each other on another Indian dish and originated new vegetable excitement . . . succulent succotash. And, in the fall, in Indian villages and on the plantations . . . the aroma of roasting ears of green corn drove appetites wild!

Rivers were rich in fish and hundreds of tempting ways of baking them, frying them, broiling them, fileting them and seasoning them were devised. And—hail the wonderful Virginia oyster! Colonial culinary magic made him King.

Virginia is the peanut capital of the world. When hogs discovered them, and fed on them, they became internationally famous as Smithfield and Virginia hams. Kings, Counts and Merchant Barons the world over have summoned them ever since!

"From Williamsburg Kitchens" is a grand collection of choice recipes in the Virginia Style. They have been gathered from culinary albums of Tidewater families, unearthed in old manuscripts and plucked from memory. These misty "pinch of this, a little of that" recipes, along with secrets of plantation kitchens, have been specially edited for the modern housewife and her kitchen. May you find in them all the savory goodness implicit in the title, "From Williamsburg Kitchens."

OMELET WITH HERBS

6 eggs
1/2 cup milk or cream
1 tsp. salt
Freshly ground pepper

3 tbsp. butter
1/2 tsp. minced chives
1/2 tsp. minced basil
1/2 tsp. minced oregano

Beat eggs until light. Stir in milk or cream, salt, and pepper. Melt butter in heavy skillet; add egg mixture; cook over low heat. As eggs begin to set, lift them gently from sides to let the uncooked portion flow underneath. Cook until eggs are thoroughly set but slightly moist in center. Sprinkle with chives, basil and oregano. Fold omelet in half; slide into hot platter. Serves 4 to 6.

CULINARY HERBS AND SPICES

HERBS

Culinary herbs are leaves of garden plants grown for seasoning food and for preparing beverages. Some culinary herbs, such as parsley, are used to garnish food dishes. Other herbs are grown for medicinal purposes or for their sweet scent.

This Cook Book gives you information about some of the more popular culinary herbs grown in Virginia. Parsley is the most popular of all culinary herbs grown. Chives has been grown for many years in Virginia but this delightful little herb deserves more attention than it is now receiving.

We have selected 14 of the many herbs grown for seasoning as we consider them among the most popular:

Anise (Pimpinella anisum). This is not Florence Fennel which is sometimes called "Sweet Anise." The seed of anise are used in flavoring candies and cookies, usually called "aniseed cookies." The seed are sometimes used in breads, cakes, apples sauces, stews, and soups. Seed are the part of the plant mainly used, but occasionally fresh leaves are used as garnish and in salads.

Sweet Basil (Ocimum basilicum). The tender fresh leaves or dry leaves are the parts used. The leaves have a clove flavor and are especially suited for tomato dishes and turtle or oxtail soups. Also the leaves are used considerably in pickling or as a garnish for salads. They are occasionally used in flavoring eggs, stews, gravies, salads, cucumbers, shrimp, sausage, or other foods.

Caraway (Carum carvi). The seed are used baked in bread, especially rye bread, and in cookies and mixed with cream or cottage cheese. They are also sometimes used in potato salad, apple pie, baked apples, and sauerkraut. When boiling cabbage or potatoes in their jackets, add a few seed. Occasionally very young tender leaves are finely chopped and added to vegetable soup and gravies.

Chives (Allium schoenoprasum). The fresh tender leaves may be used in any food that is improved by a delicate onion flavor. The chopped up fresh leaves are especially liked in salads and omelets or scrambled eggs. They are also used in soups, stews, sauces, scalloped vegetables, cottage cheese, or other foods.

Coriander (Coriandrum sativum). The dried seed are frequently sprinkled over cookies, buns, or bread or they are sugar coated as candy. Also the seed may be crushed and used in cakes, meat sauces, or ground meat. Occasionally the seed are used in poultry dressing, pickle, sausage, curries, spiced meats, and fish.

Dill (Anethum graveolens). It is said that this is the herb referred to in the Scripture as "anise." The fruiting umbels are used extensively for flavoring pickle, such as the well known dill pickle, and occasionally for vinegar. The fresh leaves are occasionally chopped up and used to flavor boiled or fried meats and fish, creamed chicken, fish sauces, and sandwiches. Also the fresh chopped up leaves are occasionally used in potato salad or boiled with cabbage, turnips, or cauliflower.

Garlic (Allium sativum). The cloves, which are obtained by separating the bulbs, are used in very small quantities in many foods where a piquant flavor suggestive of onions is desired. Among foods in which garlic is used are meats, soups, salads, pickles, omelets, sauces, or dressings. Garlic should be used in very small quantities: for example crush a small clove and rub it on the salad bowl or on roast beef before placing it in the oven or drop a small split clove into a pint of French dressing.

Sweet Marjoram (Majorana hortensis). The leaves and flowering tops of marjoram are used to flavor poultry dressing and cold meat sandwiches. also for other meats, especially veal, liver, or meat pies. Occasionally used in soups, stews, snap beans, potato salad, creamed potatoes, sausage, or egg dishes.

Parsley (Petroselinum crispum). Leaves and a small part of the stem are used as garnish for many dishes. Chopped up leaves may be sprinkled over tossed salad or used in sandwiches, soups, stews, sauces, meatloaf, boiled or creamed vegetables and other foods.

Rosemary (Rosmarinus officianalis). Use the fresh or dried leaves sparingly as flavoring for poultry, creamed soups, or leafy greens. They are also used occasionally with stews, sauces, snap beans, peas, beef, pork, or veal.

Sage (Salvia officinalis). The leaves can be used sparingly with onion for stuffing pork, ducks, or geese. The powdered leaves rubbed on the outside of fresh pork, ham, or loin give a flavor resembling that of stuffed turkey. Crushed fresh leaves may be blended with cottage or cream cheese.

Savory (Satureia hortensis). The tender leaves and stems are used fresh or dried. They may be used to flavor dressings, soups, stews, snap beans, salads, egg dishes, sauce for veal and poultry, and as a satisfying complement to many other foods.

Spearmint (Mentha spicata). Fresh sprigs of leaves are used in iced tea and other beverages. Sometimes the leaves are chopped up and sprinkled on fruit salad or used for making mint jelly.

Thyme (Thymus vulgaris). The leaves which are usually blended with other herbs, may be used in meats, poultry dressing, gravies, soups, egg dishes, cheese, or clam chowder.

SPICES

Spice—the word stirs visions of high adventure, camel caravans loaded with spices plodding across hot sands, tiny ships braving storms and unknown seas.

Today spices for which men have searched down through the centuries are to be found no farther away than our gardens or the nearest supermarket. The increased use of spices is one of the most radical changes in American cooking in the past 50 years. No longer is the imaginative cook satisfied with staple spices like pepper, cloves, cinnamon, and nutmeg.

Spices are parts of plants which are usually grown in the Tropics—"parts" meaning bark, dried leaves, seeds, stamen, shells, or any other aromatic part suitable for seasoning or preserving. Exceptions are peppers—cayenne, red, whole chili peppers, and paprika. All are prepared from the dried pod of different varieties of peppers and are grown in almost every country in the world. They have no connection with white or black pepper. Black pepper is the dried berry of a tropical climber; white pepper is obtained by removing the outer skin of the berry and using the inner portion, which is white.

Cayenne. Go easy with this one—a touch is enough! This fiery spice from Mexico and Japan is the hottest of the red peppers. It gives zing to meats and gravies. Used with restraint, it will perk up eggs, sauces, vegetables, and fish. It is one of the ingredients of curry powder.

Chili Powder. We're indebted to the ancient Aztecs for this racy blend of chili peppers and other spices. See the zip it gives cocktail sauces and eggs, gravies, stews, meat loaf, and hamburger—not forgetting that Mexican institution, chili.

Cinnamon. This spice is the bark of the cinnamon tree. However, the commercial product on the supermarket shelf is made from the bark of the cassia tree, a member of the same family, but warmer and spicier. Use whole in pickling and preserving and as flavoring for puddings and stewed fruits. Ground, this spice is a favorite in baked goods and mashed sweet potatoes.

Cloves. Native to Indonesia, wars have been fought over this warm, rich spice. Once only for the wealthy, today everyone can enjoy it. It is delicious whole for baked ham, pickling and spicy syrups; ground in baked goods, vegetables and chocolate pudding.

Curry Powder. Exotic blends of many spices, curry is the standby of Indian cookery. Wonderfully versatile, it gives an exciting pickup to leftover meats, stews, and fish dishes. Try it in French dressing . . . also with rice, shrimp, chicken, eggs, and vegetables.

Ginger. Originally from the Orient, now the pride of Jamaica, this aromatic, pungent spice is a universal favorite. Cracked, it gives zest to preserves and pickles. Ground, it perks up pot roasts, gingerbread, pies, cakes, cookies, and canned fruits.

Mace. The outer covering of the nutmeg seed, this spice is something like nutmeg in flavor, but less sharp and pungent. Ground, it's a "must" for pound cakes—delicious in chocolate dishes, too. Whole, it improves stewed fruits, fish, sauces, preserves, and pickles.

Mustard. Prized by Hippocrates as a medicine, mustard is more versatile today. Whole, it gives zing to salads, pickles and beets. Ground, it sparks sauces, meats, and gravies. Where would hot dogs and ham be without prepared mustard?

Nutmeg. European traders tried to restrict this spice to its native East Indies only to be foiled by seed-carrying birds. Nutmeg (the kernel found under the outer covering of mace) livens sauces, puddings, doughnuts, and custards. It is good in cauliflower and spinach, too.

Paprika. This is the cool and mild member of the pepper family, and a rich source of Vitamins A and C. The brilliant red color and slightly sweet taste make this spice a favorite garnish for fish, salads, meats, poultry, soups, eggs, vegetables, and cream sauces.

Poppy Seed. One of Holland's contributions to livelier cooking, these crunchy nut-like seeds are delightful used whole as a topping for breads, cakes, and cookies, and are delicious in noodles and salads. Mix with strained honey as a filling for pastries.

Saffron. This is the world's most expensive spice, but a little goes a long way. A pinch steeped in hot water gives intriguing taste and rich golden color to rice and baked goods. Saffron is a "must" in Spain's famous chicken-with-rice dish, arroz con pollo.

"On our knees grubbing in the earth,
we may not only free the plants of
choking weeds but rid ourselves of those
horrid human weeds called worries."

APPLE PIE

5 cups fresh York apples, sliced thin
2 tbsps. flour
1/2 cup white sugar
1/4 cup light brown sugar
1/4 tsp. salt

1/8 tsp. nutmeg
1/8 tsp. grated lemon rind
2 tsps. lemon juice
1 tbsp. margarine
Pastry

Mix all ingredients and heap into the lower crust. Dot with margarine and seal with the top crust. Slit crust in several places. Bake in 450°F oven 15 minutes and 350°F oven 55 minutes.

The pastry used was made from 3 cups flour, 1 cup shortening, 1 tsp. salt, and 1 cup water.

APPLE MINT JULEP

Combine 2 cups chilled apple juice
1 pint lime sherbet
A few drops mint extract

Beat until smooth and pour into tall glasses. Makes 3-4 servings. Add a sprig of mint to each glass for a pretty garnish.

BROILED CHICKEN WITH HERBS

3 broilers
1/2 tbsp. salt
1/2 tsp. pepper
1 cup butter
1 tbsp. finely chopped parsley
1/2 tsp. finely chopped sweet marjoram
1 tsp. finely chopped chives

1 leaf, finely chopped sage
1 tsp. finely chopped mint
1/4 tsp. fennel seeds
1/4 tsp. ground nutmeg
1/2 tsp. ground cinnamon
1 cup orange juice

Clean and cut broilers in half, wipe with damp cloth; season with salt and pepper. Soften butter and blend with herbs and spices. Rub herb butter over inside and outside of broilers. Broil until golden brown. Place in roaster; add orange juice and juice from broiler pan; bake covered in moderate oven (375°F), basting frequently, until tender; about 45 minutes. The orange juice imparts to the chicken a golden color and a delightful flavor. Garnish with spiced peaches or orange slices. Yield: 6 servings.

APPLE SURPRISE

1/2 cup butter or margarine	2 tsp. baking powder
1 cup sugar	2 cups cooked or canned apples
1 cup flour	1 tsp. cinnamon
1 cup milk	1/2 tsp. nutmeg

Melt butter in deep skillet or baking dish. Mix next 4 ingredients into a batter and pour this onto melted butter. Drain fruit, add spices, and spoon onto batter. Bake about 25 or 30 minutes in 350°F oven until batter covers fruit and cake browns. The fruit settles to the bottom of the pan and cake comes to top, making a delicious moist dessert. Serve plain or with cream.

BAKED TOMATOES WITH BASIL

1 qt. canned or fresh tomatoes	1/8 tsp. white pepper
1/4 tsp. salt	1 cup coarse bread crumbs
2 tsps. sugar	2 tbsps. butter or margarine
1/4 tsp. basil	

Mix tomatoes, salt, sugar, basil, and pepper. Pour into greased casserole. Sprinkle with bread crumbs; dot with butter. Bake 25 minutes in 350°F oven. If not brown, place under broiler for a few minutes. Serve.

CABBAGE WITH CARAWAY SEED BUTTER

1 medium head of cabbage	3/4 tsp. crushed marjoram leaves
1/4 cup water	3 tbsps. butter
1/2 tsp. salt	1 tsp. caraway seed

Shred entire head of cabbage. Place in a sauce pan with boiling water and salt. Cover with a tight-fitting lid and cook quickly until the cabbage is tender (approximately 10 minutes). Stir once or twice. Meanwhile, blend together the marjoram leaves, butter and caraway seed and add to cabbage. Serve hot. Makes 6 servings.

CURRIED SHRIMP ON STEAMED RICE

2 lbs. shrimp, fresh or frozen	1 cup (8 oz. can) tomato sauce
3 tbsps. butter or margarine	1 cup chicken broth
2 small onions, chopped	1/2 cup sliced, blanched almonds
1 clove garlic, minced	3 tbsps. lemon juice
1 tsp. curry powder	1/2 cup light cream
1/2 tsp. salt	

Clean shrimp. Cook fresh shrimp in a saucepan, in enough boiling water to cover, for 5 minutes. Drain. (Cook frozen shrimp as package directs; drain). Melt 2 tbsps. of the butter in a saucepan. Add onion and garlic. Cook over medium heat for about 3 minutes or until onion is transparent. Sprinkle curry powder and salt into onion mixture. Blend well. Add tomato sauce and chicken broth (canned or made with 1 chicken bouillon cube and 1 cup hot water). Simmer for 30 minutes, stirring occasionally. Meanwhile, melt remaining 1 tbsp. butter in a small skillet. Add almonds. Heat, stirring often, until toasty brown. Stir lemon juice, cream, and shrimp into sauce and heat thoroughly. Sprinkle with toasted almonds. Serve over fluffy steamed rice. Pass chutney. Makes 8 servings.

MINTED CARROTS

1 bunch (5 or 6) carrots	1 1/2 tbsps. butter or margarine
2 tsps. finely chopped fresh mint	1/3 tsp. salt

Slice carrots 1/8" thick. Cook covered in boiling salted water until almost tender. Remove cover and cook rapidly until all liquid is absorbed. Add butter and heat until butter melts. Add mint; mix lightly. Serve in hot dish at once. One-fourth teaspoon dried mint may be used, but flavor is much better when fresh mint is used.

MINTED PUNCH

1 qt. water	Juice from 6 oranges
1 1/2 cups sugar	Juice from 3 lemons
3/4 cup mint leaves, crushed	Mint for garnish

Heat water and sugar together for 5 minutes. Add mint leaves. Let stand 30 minutes; strain. Add juices, pour into tall glasses; garnish with sprigs of mint. Ginger ale may be added just before serving.

HERB S & SPICES

DROP CAKES

1/2 cup butter	2 cups oatmeal
1 cup brown sugar	2 cups flour
2 eggs	1 tsp. baking powder
1/4 cup milk	1/2 tsp. salt
1/2 cup raisins or dates, chopped or nuts, if desired	1 tsp. nutmeg

Cream butter and sugar together, add eggs and milk, then oatmeal, and gradually other dry ingredients, sifted together. Last, add dates or nuts, drop by spoonful on greased baking sheet.

DUTCH APPLE PIE

6 or 8 apples	1/2 tsp. cinnamon
1 cup brown sugar	3 tbsps. flour
1/2 cup granulated sugar	1 cup sweet or sour cream

Wash, pare and quarter apples. Mix dry ingredients together. Place half of this mixture in the bottom of an unbaked pie shell. Add apples. Mix cream with remainder of dry mixture and pour over the top. Cover with pastry. Slit crust and bake in a preheated oven (450°F) for 10 minutes. Reduce heat to 325°F and bake approximately 45 minutes or until apples are tender.

EGG-CHEESE-POTATO CASSEROLE

1 cup thin white sauce	4 hard-cooked eggs, sliced
1 tbsp. minced parsley	Soft breadcrumbs
2 cups sliced cooked potatoes	Salt, pepper
1 cup shredded cheese	

Combine white sauce and parsley. Place alternate layers of potatoes, cheese, and eggs in a greased baking dish; sprinkle with salt and pepper. Pour the white sauce over the top. Sprinkle with breadcrumbs. Bake in a moderate oven (375°F) 15 to 20 minutes. 4 servings.

HERB-FRIED CHICKEN

1 3½ lb. ready to cook frying chicken	⅛ tsp. ground white pepper
1½ tsps. salt	1 cup all purpose flour
1 tsp. paprika	Fat for frying
½ tsp. crushed tarragon	2 tbsps. water
½ tsp. ground marjoram	

Cut chicken in pieces; wash and dry. Shake flour and seasonings in paper bag. Add chicken and shake until chicken is coated with flour mixture. Heat fat in skillet with fitted cover. (A 9 inch skillet will need about ⅔ cup of melted fat.) Fry larger pieces of chicken first, slipping smaller parts around them as they brown. When chicken is lightly browned on both sides, add 2 tablespoons of water, cover tightly, and continue to brown for another 45 minutes or until chicken is very tender and shrinks from bone ends. For extra crispness, remove cover for the last 10 minutes of cooking time. Makes 4 to 5 servings.

OLD VIRGINIA APPLE COBBLER

½ lemon	2 tbsps. butter
1 cup water	Pastry:
¾ cup sugar	1 cup flour
2 tbsps. flour	½ tsp. salt
¼ tsp. nutmeg	1/3 cup shortening
3 cups apples, pared and sliced	3 tbsp. cold water

Slice lemon thin and simmer in water until rind is tender. Mix sugar, flour and nutmeg; add lemon mixture. Cook until thick. Add apples and butter and pour into a greased baking dish. Make pastry and roll thin. Cut in triangles and arrange over apple filling. Bake in 400°F oven about 40 minutes. Cobbler may be served with cream or ice cream, but it makes its own juice. This has a delightful lemon flavor.

PARSLEY SCRAMBLED EGGS

4 eggs	½ tsp. salt
4 tbsps. cream or rich milk	2 tbsps. chopped parsley

Combine eggs, cream and salt. Beat until fluffy; add parsley. Cook in heavy frying pan over moderate heat until done. Turn once. For variety add ½ cup grated sharp cheese after turning. Serve at once.

PARSLEY POTATOES

¼ cup butter or margarine	2 tbsps. finely cut parsley
4 medium-size cooked potatoes	

Melt the butter or margarine and pour over hot potatoes. Sprinkle with parsley. 4 servings.

RASPBERRY-MINT CRUSH

½ cup sugar	1 10-oz. pkg. frozen raspberries
½ cup fresh mint leaves	1 6-oz. can frozen pink lemonade
1 cup boiling water	

Combine sugar, mint leaves and boiling water. Let stand 5 minutes. Add raspberries and lemonade, stirring until thawed. Strain into chilled pitcher which is half-filled with crushed ice and add 2 cups ice water. Garnish with fresh mint leaves and berries. 9 servings.

RABBIT PIE

3 lb. rabbit dressed	1 cup diced celery in cloth bag
Parsley bouquet	1½ cups rabbit stock
Thyme bouquet	4 tbsps. butter
2 bay leaves	2½ tbsps. flour
Rosemary sprig	1 cup milk or cream

Cut rabbit into four pieces and place in 4 qt. pot. Cover with 2 qts. water and add parsley, thyme, bay leaves, rosemary and celery. Bring to boil and let simmer over medium heat 2 hours or until meat falls away from bones. Bone rabbit and cut into bite size pieces. Strain off ½ cup rabbit stock. In a 2 qt. double boiler melt butter. Stir in flour and then add the stock together with 1 cup milk or cream. Cook until the mixture comes to a boil and is smooth, stirring constantly with a wire whisk. Add celery from cloth bag and boned rabbit. Season with salt and pepper to taste. Two tablespoons of sherry or port wine may be added, if you like. Serve over batter bread cooked in a ring mold.

ROAST LAMB ROSEMARY

1 carrot, sliced	1 6-lb. leg of lamb
1 stalk celery, chopped	¾ tsp. ground rosemary
2 leeks, sliced	2 tsps. salt
1 tbsp. butter or margarine	½ tsp. ground black pepper
3 cups water	3 tbsps. flour

Heat oven to 325°F (moderately slow oven). Saute vegetables in butter for 5 minutes, stirring frequently. Stir in 1 cup of the water. Place lamb in roasting pan. Combine ¼ teaspoon of the rosemary, the salt, and black pepper. Rub this into the lamb, Add vegetable mixture. Roast, uncovered, in preheated oven for 2½ to 3 hours, or until tender. Remove roast and keep warm. Skim off excess fat from liquid in pan. Add 1¾ cups of the water and remaining ½ tsp. rosemary. Bring to a boil, then strain. Add flour, mixed with the remaining ¼ cup water. Cook, stirring, until gravy thickens. Makes 10 servings.

SPICED CIDER

1 qt. cider	½ tsp. allspice
4 sticks cinnamon	½ tsp. whole cloves

Bring cider to boil. Add spices. Let stand 4 hours. Strain. Serve hot or cold.

SPICY STEW

3 tbsps. shortening	6 crushed coriander seeds
2 tbsps. flour	1 qt. water
2 tsps. salt	2 cups diced onions
4 tsps. paprika	3 cups diced carrots
2 lbs. chuck or beef, cut in 1" cubes	3 cups diced potatoes
1 clove garlic, minced	4 tomatoes, diced
1 bay leaf	½ tsp. caraway seed

Heat shortening in Dutch oven or deep, heavy kettle with tight cover. Combine flour, salt and paprika. Dip meat into flour mixture, coating each piece well. Brown meat and garlic in hot shortening, turning to brown all sides. Add remaining ingredients. Cover and cook slowly for 1½ hours, adding a little more water from time to time as needed to keep the goulash moist, but not soupy. Remove bay leaf, serve piping hot. Makes 6 generous servings.

POUND CAKE WITH MACE

2 cups butter
2 cups sugar
9 eggs
4 cups sifted cake flour

1 tsp. vanilla
$1/2$ tsp. mace
$1/2$ tsp. cream of tartar
$1/2$ tsp. salt

Cream butter thoroughly. Slowly dribble in sugar, beating and cream-ing well. Beat in eggs 1 at a time. Add vanilla and mace. Sift flour with cream of tartar and salt; add slowly, beating at low speed until thoroughly blended. Pour into 2 greased loaf pans lined with waxed paper, or into 1 large tube pan. Bake at 325°F for 1 hour.

ROAST BEEF WITH HERBS

$1/4$ tsp. basil
$1/4$ tsp. pepper
1 can cream of mushroom soup
Heavy foil to wrap

$1/4$ tsp. rosemary
3-4 lbs. roast chuck
1 pk. dried onion soup

Place dried onion soup in center of foil. Place roast on top. Pour undi-luted soup and herbs on top. Bring up foil around roast; close tightly in sandwich fold. Cook in 325°F oven, allowing one hour per pound of meat. Meat and gravy have a delicious flavor, a deep brown color. The herbs in the onion soup mix gives this roast its flavor.

SPICY BAKED ACORN SQUASH

2 large acorn squash
2 tbsps. brown sugar
4 tsps. butter or margarine
$1/2$ tsp. salt

$1/8$ tsp. black pepper
$1/4$ tsp. ground cinnamon
8 whole cloves

Heat oven to 400°F (moderately hot). Wash squash and cut in half lengthwise. Scrape out seeds and stringy portion. Blend together brown sugar, butter, salt, pepper and cinnamon. Put one-fourth of the mixture in the center of each squash half. Stick a whole clove in the ends of squash. Bake covered in preheated oven for 45 minutes. Uncover and continue to bake for 15 minutes, or until squash is tender. Makes 4 servings.

STUFFED POTATOES CREOLE

6 baking potatoes
1 medium green pepper, diced
1/3 cup butter or margarine
2 tbsps. instant minced onion
1 medium tomato, diced
1 to 2 tbsp. milk

2 tsps. salt
1/4 tsp. ground white pepper
1 tsp. paprika
1/4 tsp. crumbled whole rosemary
   leaves
Paprika for garnish

Wash potatoes. Dry. Bake in a preheated oven (450°F) 1 hour or until done. In the meantime, saute green pepper in 3 tbsps. of the butter until limp. Add onion and tomato and cook 1 minute longer. Cut potatoes in half length-wise and scoop out centers, leaving shells intact. Add milk and seasonings to potato centers and mash well. Blend in sauted vegetables. Fill shells with mixture and dot tops with remaining butter. Bake in a preheated hot oven (400°F) 20 minutes. Serve at once, garnished with paprika.

VEAL PAPRIKA

8 slices bacon, diced
1/4 cup chopped onion
1/4 cup flour
2 tsps. salt
1/4 tsp. pepper
2 lbs. boneless veal shoulder,
   cut in 1" cubes
1/4 cup water
1 tbsp. paprika

1 cup dairy sour cream
8 oz. elbow macaroni
2 tbsps. butter
1 tsp. poppy seed
1 4-oz. can sliced mushrooms and
   liquid
1 tsp. paprika
2 tbsps. chopped parsley

Fry bacon until crisp; add onion and fry until transparent. Remove from skillet. Mix flour, salt, and pepper in paper sack. Dust veal with seasoned flour by shaking in sack. Brown lightly. Add water and bacon and onion mixture. Cover and simmer until fork-tender, 50 to 60 minutes. Stir in paprika and sour cream. Meanwhile, cook macaroni in boiling salted water; drain, and toss with butter, poppy seed and mushrooms. Reserve a few mushrooms for garnish. Pour macaroni mixture into lightly-greased shallow 2-quart baking dish. Pour veal mixture on top, and add remaining mushrooms, parsley, and paprika. Place in moderate oven (350°F) for about 15 minutes to heat thoroughly. Garnish with parsley. Makes 4-6 servings.

SPICY BAKED HAM SLICE

Slice of ham, 1-inch thick
1/4 cup brown sugar
1/8 tsp. allspice
1/4 tsp. ground ginger
1/8 tsp. cinnamon

3/4 cup canned peach juice
3 whole cloves
2 tsp. cornstarch
1 tbsp. cold water

Trim fat around the edge of ham and score every two inches so the slice doesn't curl while cooking. Rub brown sugar into the top of the ham slice and place in a shallow baking dish. Stir a little peach juice into the ground spices to make a smooth mixture. Slowly add the rest of the juice and cloves and pour around ham slice. Bake at 325 degrees about an hour, basting occasionally with the juices that accumulate in the pan. When the ham is done, remove from the pan to a warm serving platter. Add blended water and cornstarch to the liquid to make a sauce to serve with the ham. Cook sauce over low heat until it boils and thickens.

JAM CAKE

1 cup butter
1 1/2 cups of sugar
4 eggs
1 cup buttermilk
1 tsp. soda

1 cup jam (strawberry is good)
3 cups of flour
1 1/2 tsp. cinnamon
1 1/2 tsp. allspice
1 tsp. clove

Cream butter and sugar until it is light and fluffy. Add eggs, one at a time and beat well. Dissolve soda in buttermilk and add to creamed mixture alternately with flour. Fold in jam. Bake in greased and floured pans, at 350 degrees about half an hour. Check to see if the center springs back when touched.

SHRIMP BISQUE

1 lb. cooked shrimp — put through meat grinder
1 qt. of milk
1/2 cup of heavy cream
Salt and pepper to taste

3 rounded tablespoons of flour
1/2 stick of butter
1 dessert spoon A1 and Worcestershire sauce
3/4 cup sherry

Method: Melt butter in saucepan, stir flour in slowly until well blended and smooth. Add milk slowly. Stir slowly so as not to lump, until have thick sauce. Add shrimp, add cream, add seasoning, add sherry last after soup is good and hot and smooth. Warm soup plates, place thin slice lemon in plate. Sprinkle lightly with paprika.

POTATO AND HAM CHOWDER

1/4 cup finely chopped onion
1 tbsp. butter or margarine
1 cup diced raw potato
1/2 cup coarsely chopped cooked smoked ham
1 tsp. salt
1 tsp. Worcestershire sauce
Thyme

Few grains paprika
1/8 tsp. celery salt
1 1/2 cups boiling water
2 cups hot milk
1 tbsp. flour
2 tbsps. water
1/3 cup cooked peas

Cook onion in butter or margarine until it is golden brown. Combine onion, potato, ham, seasonings, and boiling water and cook 15 minutes. Add hot milk. Blend water with flour, stirring until smooth. Stir into the vegetable-and-meat mixture. Cook gently until slightly thickened. Add peas, and heat. 4 servings.

HORS D'OEUVRES and APPETIZERS

VIRGINIA HAM STRAWS

2 cups flour
2 level tsp. baking powder
½ tsp. salt
½ cup milk
¾ cup ground Virginia ham

½ cup butter
¼ tsp. Paprika
⅛ tsp. red pepper
1 egg

Sift dry ingredients three or four times, cut in butter, add whole egg without beating and stir in, add milk and ham and mix well. Roll very thin, cut in strips about ¼ inch wide and four inches long and lay in rows in buttered pan about ¾ inch apart. Bake in moderate oven until pale brown. Serve with salads, soups, or breakfast coffee.

HOT VIRGINIA DIP

1 cup chopped pecans
2 tsp. butter
16 oz. cream cheese, softened
4 tablespoons milk

5 ounces dried beef, cut fine
1 tsp. garlic salt
1 cup sour cream
4 teaspoons minced green onions

Saute pecans in butter and set aside. Mix all other ingredients thoroughly. Place in a 1 1/2 quart baking dish, and top with pecans. Bake at 350 for 20 minutes. Serve with small bread sticks.

SHRIMPY DIPPY

16 oz. cream cheese, softened
1/2 tbsp. onion, minced
1 tsp. lemon juice

1 cup cooked shrimp, cut fine
2 dashes curry powder
3 tbsp. minced chutney

Mix all ingredients well. Serve with favorite crackers.

HOT CRAB DIP

1 lb. picked crabmeat
1 tbsp. horseradish
2 tbsp. capers
2 cups mayonnaise
1 tsp. lemon rind, grated

1/4 tsp. salt
1/2 tsp. garlic powder
2 dashes of Tabasco
1 tsp. Worcestershire

Preheat oven to 350 degrees. Mix all ingredients well, and pour into a greased 2 quart casserole. Bake 25 - 30 minutes. Serve hot with Melba rounds, toast or large crackers.

EXCELLENT EASY IDEAS FOR ENTERTAINING

Wrap cantaloupe and honeydew melon balls in thin strips of Smithfield ham and secure with toothpicks.

Wrap half slices of lean bacon around an assortment of oysters, scallops, water chestnuts and livers, and bake in a hot oven until crisp. Drain and serve while warm.

Hollow a red cabbage and fill with the cheese dip of your choice. Arrange a tray of colorful vegetables such as sliced raw squash, zucchini, carrots, celery, mushrooms and cucumbers around the dip.

HORS D'OEUVRES
and APPETIZERS

CHEESE BALLS

2 ozs. cream cheese
4 ozs. bleu cheese
4 ozs. sharp cheese
1 clove of garlic

1 tps. Worcestershire sauce
¾ cup parsley, chopped
¾ cup nuts, chopped

Mix the cheese, garlic, worcestershire sauce and half the parsley and nuts, shape into a ball and roll in the other half of the parsley and nut mixture. Place in the center of a tray and surround with sliced party rye bread three-quarters of the way around, and with triangle thins or other crisp crackers one-third of the circle. Arrange cocktail spreaders around the tray.

CHEESE BALL

1 large package Philadelphia cream cheese
¼ lb. bleu cheese
1 tbsp. sour cream

Grated onion   )
Garlic powder   )   to taste
Worcestershire sauce)

Form into a ball and roll in chopped nuts or parsley.

CHEESE DIP

1 wedge bleu cheese (1 oz. or more) to taste
1 small pkg. of cream cheese

Cream the latter until consistency of whipped cream, using milk or light cream. Add crumbled bleu cheese and mix well.

Add—dash of garlic salt; few drops of Worcestershire sauce; few drops of lemon juice and onion juice to taste.

Excellent on potato chips or crackers.

23

CHEESE DIP

1 6-oz. pkg. chive cream cheese
2 tbsps. mayonnaise
1 tsp. prepared mustard
1 tsp. Worcestershire sauce

2 chopped hard boiled eggs
1/4 cup milk
Salt and pepper

Several hours ahead beat cheese and stir in mayonnaise, mustard. Now sauce, salt and pepper. Add eggs, mix well, beat in milk until good dip consistency. Refrigerate. Remove from refrigerator 1/2 hour before serving and sprinkle with chopped parsley.

CHEESE SPREAD

1/2 lb. cream cheese
1/4 lb. roquefort or bleu cheese

1/2 clove of garlic mashed handful of minced chives salt and pepper to taste

Mix together 24 hours before you use it, if possible. If it should dry out, moisten with 1 teaspoon of Bourbon.

CLAM MIX

1 can minced clams
1 wedge cream cheese

Onion salt
Worcestershire sauce

Cream cheese until soft, add drained clams and mix well, flavor to taste. Place mix in center of cheese plate, surround with your favorite crackers. You have a subtle dish that sends your guests guessing and exclaiming.

COCKTAIL SPREAD

1 small onion
2 pkgs. cream cheese
3 hard boiled eggs
4 med. sized sweet pickles

2 pimentos
2 tbsp. mayonnaise
1/4 cup butter or margarine
Salt, pepper, paprika

Put through the coarse chopper, eggs, pickles, pimentos, and onion. Mash cream cheese and blend with mayonnaise. Season with salt, pepper and paprika to taste. Combine the two mixtures and add melted butter or margarine. Chill.

HORS D'OEUVRES and APPETIZERS

HOT TOASTED CHEESE CANAPE

2 cups grated cheese
1 egg well beaten
6 dashes Tabasco sauce
1 tsp. Lea & Perrins

1 tbsp. tomato ketchup
1/2 tsp. salt (scant)
2 loaves bread
1/2 lb. bacon

Mix with fork, cheese, egg & seasonings. Remove bread crusts and cut in desired shapes. Spread with cheese & egg mixture. Top with thin, medium size pieces of bacon. Toast in oven 450°F until brown. These may be prepared days in advance and put in freezer until a few minutes before toasting.

MARINATED SHRIMP

4 lbs. peeled cooked shrimp
1 cup Wesson oil
1 cup tarragon vinegar

2 cloves of garlic
2 medium onions
Salt, black pepper and red pepper

Mix shrimp, Wesson oil and vinegar to which garlic have been crushed with salt, black pepper and red pepper. Slice onions thin, place over shrimp in bowl. Marinate in refrigerator overnight. Drain most of juice off, place in bowl, serve with toothpicks and crackers as an hors d'oeuvre.

MOCK TERRAPIN

1 lb. chipped beef
2 cups canned tomatoes
1/4 or 1/2 cup cheese to taste
2 tbsps. minced onion

2 tbsps. minced green pepper
1 tbsp. flour (heaping)
2 hard boiled eggs

Simmer onion & green pepper in 3 tbsp. fat until tender & slightly brown. Add beef, cook 2 or 3 min. Add flour, blend with fat, add milk. Bring to boil, stirring constantly. Add tomato and cheese. Let stand on low heat for short time. Two hard boiled eggs may be sliced into this when ready to serve or two slightly beaten eggs may be stirred into mixture and poured immediately into serving dish.

BEEFY OLIVE SPREAD

8 oz. creamed cheese, softened	2 tbsp. mayonnaise
1 tsp. dry minced onion	3/4 stuffed green olives
1 tbsp. dry sherry	4 oz. dried beef, minced

Chop olives and soak dried onion in the sherry to soften. Blend cheese and mayonnaise. Add onion, beef and olives. Chill and serve with assorted crackers. Serves 15 to 20.

MARINATED MUSHROOMS

36 fresh small mushrooms	2 tbsp. parsley flakes
1/2 oz. package garlic salad dressing mix	2 tbsp. spoons garlic powder
1/2 cup lemon juice	1 1/2 cups vegetable oil
	salt and pepper to taste

Clean mushrooms and remove stems. Cover in salt water and boil 1 minute. Drain well. Mix all ingredients and pour over caps. Chill at least 24 hours. Drain and serve cold.

CRABBY MUSHROOMS

36 fresh medium mushrooms	1 tsp. capers, chopped
1/2 lb. fresh crabmeat	1/4 teaspoon dry mustard
1 tbsp. parsley, chopped	1/2 cup mayonnaise
1 tbsp. pimento, chopped	Parmesan cheese

Preheat oven to 375. Remove stems and discard. Mix other ingredients, stuff caps and sprinkle with cheese. Bake for 10 minutes. Yields 36.

Hors D' oeuvres and appetizers were not offered during colonial times. These companions to the cocktail came in with prohibition to accompany drinks that were often unpalatable. This first course is enjoyed by modern gastronomes along with good conversation.

HORS D'OEUVRES and APPETIZERS

HOT OLIVE CHEESE PUFFS

1 cup graded sharp cheese
3 tbsps. soft butter
1/2 cup sifted flour

1/4 tsp. salt
2 dashes red pepper

Mix all ingredients well. Wrap each stuffed olive in about 1 teaspoon of the cheese dough, completely covering olive, wrap and freeze. To serve unwrap desired number of frozen puffs, arrange on ungreased pan and bake at 400°F 10 to 15 minutes. Serve hot. They do not have to be frozen, it is easier to have them prepared ahead of time.

SHRIMP IN HOT FRENCH DRESSING

1 lump of butter
3 tbsps. Wesson oil
1 scant tablespoon vinegar

1 tsp. Worcestershire sauce
Pepper, salt and mustard

Mix all ingredients well, heat, add cooked picked shrimp, medium amount.

SHRIMP PATE

4 lbs. fresh shrimp
2 medium onions
1/2 cup melted butter
3 tbsps. lemon juice

1/2 cup mayonnaise
Salt, pepper & dry mustard (to taste)
1/2 cup brandy

Shell, clean and cook shrimp. Mash very fine in a big bowl with a potato masher, adding minced onion as you do it. When you can mash no more, pour in butter, mixing thoroughly. Add lemon juice & mayonnaise and continue to pound. It will be a stiff paste. Add seasoning & brandy and mix again. Pack mixture in mold & press down well. Chill at least 12 hours in refrigerator. When ready to serve, turn out and slice with a thin, hot sharp knife. This can be kept indefinitely in refrigerator.

BACON ROLL UPS

1 1/2 cups herb stuffing mix	8-10 oz. bacon
1/2 cup water	1/4 lb. sausage
1/4 cup butter	1 egg slightly beaten

Heat water and melt butter in it. Remove from heat and add stuffing, egg and sausage. Chill 1 hour. Preheat oven to 375 degrees. Shape mixture into bite size balls. Divide bacon strips into thirds. Wrap around mixture and secure with toothpicks. Bake in shallow pan for 35 minutes, turning once. Drain on paper towels and serve hot. Serves 30.

SAUCE FOR SHRIMP OR CRAB MEAT

1 cup olive oil	dash tabasco
1 bottle horseradish	1/2 cup vinegar
1 bottle catsup	1 tsp. paprika
1 tsp. salt	1 scrapped onion
1/2 tsp. red pepper	1 tbsp. Worcestershire sauce
1/2 cup lemon juice	

Combine ingredients and serve with cooked shrimp or crab meat.

SHRIMP CUCUMBER CUPS

1 large cucumber
Shrimp
Lettuce Hearts

Sauce: Ketchup or Chili sauce with enough horseradish to make sharp taste.

Cut cucumbers into pieces 1 1/2 inches long, removing skin and making striped effect. Scoop centers out, put in a little of the sauce and pile the shrimp on top. Serve on slices of lettuce hearts, garnish shrimp with more sauce and parsley flakes.

Fresh pineapple is a Virginia favorite dating to Colonial Days when the ships returned from the Caribbean with luscious fruits. Sea captains would put a pineapple on their gate post to let friends and neighbors know that they were welcome. Today's hostess serves a fresh pineapple boat filled with a cheese ball and arranges trays of fruits and cheeses for guests to slice and serve.

SOUPS, CHOWDERS and STEWS

CLAM CHOWDER

1 qt. quahog or cherry stone clams shelled	2 tbsp. flour
1 medium onion, juice or chopped	4 saltine crackers
4 small slices fat pork	1/2 pt. heavy cream
	1/2 pt. coffee cream

Chop clams, keep cool until needed. Strain juice carefully to avoid sand. Simmer pork and onion together until fat is melted. Add flour enough to absorb fat. Add clam juice and crushed crackers. This may be set aside on stove if desired.

One-half hour before serving, add clams and stir until cooked. Add cream. Serve at once.

CLAM CHOWDER (with fresh clams)

1/4 lb. Salt Pork	1 qt. Chopped Clams
1 Large Onion	1/8 lb. Butter
3 Medium Sized Potatoes	Salt and Pepper
3 Cups Milk	

Cut salt pork into small dices and render in sauce pan. Reserve the craklins. Cook in the fat 1 large onion, thinly sliced, until golden. Cook in 2 qt. pan with 1½ cups of water 3 medium sized potatoes (peeled and cubed) for ten minutes. Drain liquor from potatoes into 4 qt. pan. Add 1 qt. of chopped clams. Cook for 25 min. Then add 3 cups of milk, cracklings, potatoes, onion, butter and salt and pepper to taste. Serve in soup bowls with dot crackers. Serves 8.

FISH CHOWDER

4 lb. cod or haddock in one piece

4 slices lean salt pork

4 white potatoes

2 large white onions

Lump of butter

1 pt. rich milk

Salt & pepper

Cover fish with water, season, let come to boil. Remove from fire and strain, saving liquor. Dry out pork in skillet, drain, cut pork in cubes. Pare & slice thin, potatoes and onions, add these to the fish liquor bring to boil. Cook 10 minutes. Remove skin and bones without mashing fish, add to liquor. Boil 2 minutes only. Add butter and milk. Bring to boil, cover and remove from fire. Have toasted crackers or pilot crackers to add to chowder when it is served. Serves eight.

FRENCH ONION SOUP

4 medium onions

1 tbsp. butter

1 qt. brown stock (concentrated, or four boullion cubes)

1/2 tsp. Worcestershire sauce

Salt and pepper

Rounds of toast

Grated Parmesan cheese

Slice onions thin and brown in butter. Add broth, sauce, salt and pepper; simmer until onions are tender. Pour soup into a casserole. Arrange toast on top, sprinkle with grated cheese, and place under broiler until cheese melts and browns. Rub casserole or toast with cut clove of garlic. Serve 4.

KIDNEY SOUP

1 beef kidney

1 lb. beef for stock

Flour

Pepper

Salt

1 large onion

2 stalks celery

2 carrots

2 qts. water

Soak kidney in cold, slightly salted, water for 1/2 hr. Make stock with celery, onion and beef, salt and pepper. Cut kidney into small pieces and roll in the flour. Put 2 tbsp. dripping into a pan and brown kidney. Add this to stock together with the grated carrots and cook until tender. Remove beef stock and celery. If a thicker soup is desired, mix some flour into water add to soup. A little Kitchen Bouquet improves color.

SOUPS, CHOWDERS and STEWS

CONFEDERATE BEEF STEW

2 lbs. lean stew beef	1 bay leaf
2 tbsp. salad oil	1/8 tsp. thyme
1 lg. apple, shredded	4 tsp. cornstarch
1 med. carrot, shredded	1/4 cup cold water
1/2 med. onion, sliced	1/4 tsp. Kitchen Bouquet
1/3 cup dry red wine	1 clove garlic, minced
2 beef bouillon cubes	2 1/2 cups egg noodles, cooked
1/4 tsp. poppy seeds	

Cut meat into 1 inch cubes and brown well in hot oil. Add apple, carrot, onion, water, wine, garlic, bouillon cubes, bay leaf and thyme. Cover and cook over low heat for about 2 hours or until beef is tender. Remove the bay leaf. Combine cornstarch and cold water and add to the beef mixture. Stir while cooking until mixture thickens. Stir in Kitchen Bouquet. Serve over drained noodles. Sprinkle with poppy seeds. Serves 6.

CRAB BISQUE

1 can green pea soup	2 cups whole milk
1 can tomato soup	1 lb. crab meat
1 can mushroom soup	

Heat to boiling, add 1 lb. crab meat. Let get very hot, take off stove and add 1 tablespoon sherry to each serving.

CREAM OF GREEN PEPPER SOUP

1 medium green pepper, chopped	1 can (10 1/2 ozs.) condensed cream of
1/2 small onion, chopped	celery soup
2 tbsps. butter	1 soup can of milk

Heat pepper and onion in butter. Cook 5 minutes. Place pepper mixture in electric blender and blend well. Add cream of celery soup and milk, blend few seconds until smooth. Heat soup gently.

CLAM CHOWDER

1 qt. clams	3 cups potatoes, diced
1 1/3 cups onion, chopped	Salt and white pepper to taste
1/3 cup salt pork or bacon fat	

Clean and chop clams to desired size. Add onions to clams. Cover with water (or clam juice), add fat drippings or cubed pork and cook 30 minutes or until tender. Then add potatoes; let come to boil. Cook until potatoes are creamy. Serves six.

CREAM OF MUSHROOM SOUP

1/2 lb. mushrooms	3 cups milk
2 cups water	1 cup cream
Salt & pepper	Flour to thicken
1 tbsp. butter	

Peel & put mushrooms thru food chopper. Put in double boiler & cover with 2 cups water. Add salt & pepper & simmer 1 hr. then add rest of ingredients & thicken with flour and water. Boil until creamy. Add dash of paprika and serve.

YORKTOWN CRAB SOUP

1/3 cup butter	1/2 tsp. fresh parsley
1 tbsp. flour	1/2 pint milk
1/2 tsp. salt	2 cups crabmeat
1/8 tsp. red pepper	3/4 pint cream
1/8 tsp. nutmeg	1/4 cup sherry
1/8 tsp. mace	

Melt butter in the top of a double boiler. Add flour, seasonings and milk. Stir constantly until mixture thickens. Add crabmeat, stirring constantly. When almost ready to serve, add cream and sherry. Serves 6.

SOUPS, CHOWDERS and STEWS

NAVY BEAN SOUP

1/2 lb. dry navy beans
water to cover (cold)
1 pt. boiling water
1 oz. bacon or salt pork
2 tsps. chopped onions

2/3 cup tomatoes
1 tsp. sugar
1/4 tsp. dry mustard
Salt and pepper to taste

Wash beans thoroughly. Soak in cold water about six hours. Do not drain. Add boiling water to cover and heat to boiling temperature. Simmer about one hour until tender, but not mushy. Cut bacon in small pieces and fry together with onions until lightly browned. Add tomatoes, sugar, mustard, salt and pepper to bacon mixture. Combine tomato-bacon mixture with beans, cook for 20 to 30 minutes more and serve.

BRUNSWICK STEW

1 qt. boiling water
1 pt. chopped tomatoes
1 hen or two small chickens
3 slices bacon
2 med. onions
6 ears of corn cut from
cob or one can corn

1 cup fine bread crumbs
1 tsp. salt
1/2 tsp. brown sugar
1/2 tsp. white pepper
1/2 pod red pepper
1 tsp. worcestershire sauce

Place the onions, chopped fine, tomatoes skinned, and cut in small pieces, the bacon and jointed chicken into a large soup pot. Add water and let the mixture simmer until tender. Remove the chicken from the liquor. When cool enough to handle, cut the meat from the bones and chop or cut into bite size pieces. Return to kettle, add corn and boil 20 minutes. Add stock, bread crumbs, sugar, salt and pepper. Serves 10 to 12.

"Chowders were probably the common ancestors of the more refined soups. The word chowder comes from the French word for caldron, chaudiere. Chowders originated as a community fish stew to which each neighbor contributed something. These contributions were all cooked together in a common caldron."

OYSTER SOUP

1 pt. oysters
1 pt. milk
1 tsp. butter
1 tsp. flour

1 tsp. chopped parsley
A little cayenne pepper
Salt

Put oysters into a saucepan with pepper and salt. Cover at once and cook until gills of oysters begin to curl. Heat the milk and add flour and butter which have been creamed together. Add to oysters slowly and serve immediately. Sprinkle parsley into the oysters just before serving. A beaten egg added to the soup before serving is a great addition.

PLANTATION PEANUT SOUP

2 cups chicken broth
1 tsp. chopped onion
2 tbsps. butter
1 tbsp. chopped celery
1 tbsp. flour

5 tbsps. peanut butter
4 tbsps. ground peanuts
1/8 tsp. celery salt
1/2 tsp. salt
1/2 tsp. lemon juice

Melt butter in heavy sauce pan and add diced onion and celery. Saute 5 minutes but do not brown. Add flour and blend well. Stir in hot chicken broth and cook 30 minutes. Remove from fire, strain, and add peanut butter, celery salt, salt and lemon juice. Return to fire until mixture reaches boiling point. Remove from fire, sprinkle with ground peanuts just before serving. Serves 4 to 6.

POTATO AND FISH CHOWDER

1/2 lb. fillets of cod, haddock, or other
white fish, cut in small pieces
1 cup diced raw potato
3/4 cup diced raw carrots
2 cups water
2 ozs. salt pork, diced

1/4 cup chopped onion
1 1/2 tbsps. flour
1 cup milk
1 1/4 tsps. salt
1/4 tsp. Worcestershire sauce
Pepper

Cook fish, potatoes, and carrots in the water for about 15 minutes. Do not drain. Cook the salt pork in a fry pan until crisp; remove from pan. Add the onion to the fat and cook for a few minutes. Blend in the flour and add the milk. Combine with the fish and vegetables and add seasonings. Simmer for 10 minutes, stirring frequently. Garnish with the salt pork crumbled very fine. 4 servings.

SOUPS, CHOWDERS and STEWS

CORN CHOWDER

3 slices of bacon
1 med. onions, sliced
4 med. potatoes, sliced
6 soda cracker

2 cups of milk
2 cups cooked corn
1 tsp. salt
1/4 tsp. pepper

Brown bacon until crisp in a large saucepan. Add onions and cook until clear and lightly browned on edges. Add potatoes and water and cook until potatoes are tender. Soak crackers in milk. Add corn, salt, pepper and soaked crackers to the cooked potato mixture. Heat to the boiling point. Serves 4.

YORKTOWN ONION SOUP

1/4 cup butter
3 cups onions, thinly sliced
Three 10 3/4 oz. cans of beef bullion
1 1/2 cans water

1 tbsp. cornstarch
1/4 cup water
1/4 cup sour cream
1 tbsp. sugar

Melt butter in 2 quart pot and saute onions until clear. Add bouillon, water and sugar. Cover and cook on low for about half an hour. Mix cornstarch and water to make a thin paste and add to soup to thicken slightly, stirring constantly. Serves 6.

QUICK POTATO SOUP

2 cups thinly sliced raw potatoes	1 tbsp. butter or margarine
1/4 cup finely chopped onion	1/4 tsp. Worcestershire sauce
1 1/4 cups boiling water	1 tsp. salt
1 1/2 cups milk	Pepper

Add potatoes and onion to the boiling water. Cover and cook for 15 to 20 minutes, or until potatoes are tender. Mash the potatoes slightly with a fork to thicken the soup a little if desired. Add milk, butter or margarine and seasonings. Heat. For a touch of color, garnish each serving with chopped parsley, grated cheese, croutons, diced crisp bacon, or finely cut watercress or chives.

4 servings, 1 cup each.

SEAFOOD CHOWDER

1 lb. white fish filet chunks	1 tsp. red pepper flakes, nutmeg or
6 strips bacon	mace
2 potatoes diced	1 can celery soup
1 large onion diced	1 can cond. clam chowder (no to-
1 tbsp. chopped parsley	matoes)

Fry bacon and put aside. Saute potatoes, vegetables and spices, then add cans soup and potatoes and cook until potatoes are done. Add fish sauce and cook 10 min. Add crumbled bacon and serve.

SHRIMP BISQUE

2 cups fresh cooked shrimp	2 tbsps. flour
1 cup Shayis, Hock, Sauterne or any	1/4 cup butter
other white wine	1 cup cream
2 tbsps. onion, minced	1/2 cup mushrooms, chopped, cooked
1/4 cup celery chopped fine	Salt & pepper
2 cups milk	

Clean shrimp and chop fine. Cook celery and onion in the butter gently for about 5 min. Add flour and blend. Gradually add the milk & cook stirring constantly until thick. Add shrimp, mushrooms, cream, wine and seasonings.

The 1 cup of cream may be substituted for 1 cup of milk, then garnish with some whipped cream and a dash of paprika.

SOUPS, CHOWDERS and STEWS

SHRIMP BISQUE

1 pt. milk	1 tbsp. flour mixed to a paste with a
1 cup cream	little milk
Juice and grated rind of 1 lemon	1 pt. of shrimp, cooked and broken
2 egg yolks	(not cut) into pieces

Put milk in double boiler, when it comes to a boil, add cream, lemon juice and rind, egg yolks, flour paste and shrimp, season with salt, red and black pepper then sherry. Serve hot.

SPLIT PEA SOUP

1 lb. split peas	Celery and tops
Hambone	Salt and pepper
Onion	

Wash the peas and put them in large kettle with three quarts of cold water and hambone, one cut up onion and some chopped up celery tops. Simmer about three hours. Remove the bone and put the soup through a strainer. Chill the soup and remove layer of grease, if any. Flavor with salt and pepper. Serve hot. Good with cereal crunch for croutons.

VICHYSOISE SOUP (Cold Potato Soup)

1 medium sized onion	2 qts. chicken broth
2 leeks or green onions	1 cup heavy cream
2 tbsps. butter	1/4 cup chopped chives
2 tbsps. flour	Nutmeg
4 medium sized potatoes	Salt

Peel and slice onions and leeks very thin; saute in butter until faintly brown. Blend in flour, but do not brown. Add pared potatoes and broth and cook 40 minutes or until the potatoes are very soft. Force through sieve & cool. Add cream and cool to room temperature, sprinkle with chopped chives, salt and nutmeg. Yields six portions.

OYSTER AND SPINACH CREAM SOUP

1 quart oysters
I lb. frozen spinach, chopped
3 tbsp. butter
1/3 cup chopped onion
1 rib celery, finely chopped
3 tbsp. all-purpose flour
pinch of nutmeg

1/4 tsp. garlic salt
1 tbsp. steak sauce
2 cups milk
2 cups half and half
 cream
salt and pepper

Cook oysters with liquid in 2 cups of water until firm. Drain and keep oyster stock hot. Puree oysters in blender. Cook spinach and drain well. Puree in blender. Melt butter over medium heat. Cook onions and celery stirring constantly. Add flour and stir constantly to make a smooth paste. Pour in hot oyster stock, stirring constantly. Cook over low heat for about 30 minutes. Strain mixture and return to heat. Add pureed oysters and spinach to simmering liquid. Add garlic salt, nutmeg, steak sauce. Salt and pepper to taste. Serves 6.

PUREE MONGOLE

1 cup split peas
5 cups water
2 cups tomato juice
2 tbsps. butter or margarine

1 onion
1 cup cream
Salt and pepper

Soak split peas overnight in plenty of water to cover. Drain in morning. Combine the five cups of water with peas, tomato juice, salt and pepper to taste. Fry onion which has been minced in two tbsp. butter or margarine until onion is soft and yellow. Add to first mixture. Bring all to boil and simmer about 4-5 min. or until peas are soft. Add more seasoning if desired. Strain soup to remove pea husks. Add cream and bring to boil again. Place a dash of paprika on top before serving.

The eighteenth-century citizens of Williamsburg were admirers of good soup. Tidewater Virginians, being mostly of English and Scottish stock, continued the English custom of thick soups. When asked for the secret of today's good soups, the chef at the Williamsburg Inn for many years replied, "It's the way the ingredients are put together and the seasonings".

BEVERAGES

WASSAIL

2 qt. apple juice or cider
2 sticks cinnamon
10 whole cloves
1 small nutmeg
1 piece ginger root (optional)
2 oranges (juice)
2 lemons (juice)
1 tbsp. brown sugar

Simmer apple juice or cider with
spices for three hours. Add juice
of oranges, lemons and sugar.
Serve hot from large bowl (may
be made in advance & reheated),
with fruit cake or assorted cookies.

FROSTY FRUIT DRINK

1 cup crushed strawberries and juice
1/2 cup orange juice
1/3 cup lemon juice

About 1/2 cup sugar
1/4 tsp. salt
4 cups milk

Combine the chilled ingredients and beat with rotary egg beater. Chill. Serves 4-5.

FRUIT PUNCH

1 qt. of gingerale
1 large can pineapple juice
1 large bottle grape juice

1 can frozen orange juice, diluted
1 can frozen lemonade, diluted

Excellent for a crowd of unknown size because it can be made as needed without fear of waste. Provide sufficient ice for maximum number expected. A frozen ring mold or floating sherbet (made with a water base) is a great addition to appearance.

This recipe makes 5½ quarts: 40 4 oz. servings.

FRUITED ICED TEA

Boil for 5 minutes: 4 qts. water
                    3 cups sugar
Add 5 tsps. tea and steep for 5 minutes
Add: 1 can frozen lemon juice
     1 can frozen orange juice, small size
     A few mint leaves or pinch of Allspice
Strain and chill
Makes about 4½ quarts.

FRUIT PUNCH

3 cups orange juice
rind of 1 orange
1/4 cup lemon juice
rind of 1 lemon
1 cup pineapple juice
3 cups water

6 cloves
1/2 tsp. cinnamon
1/2 tsp. cloves (whole)
1/2 tsp. allspice (whole)
2 qts. gingerale
mint sprigs

Combine fruit juices and rinds with water, and add spices. Stir and let stand several hours at room temperature. Strain out spices—use fine cheese cloth. Pour over ice in punch bowl. Add gingerale and mint to garnish. Serves 25-30.

BEVERAGES

APPLE JUICE SPARKLE

Mix equal parts of apple juice and ginger ale. Pour over ice and serve at once.

ARRACK PUNCH

2 large oranges
¾ lb. loaf-sugar
1 qt. boiling water

1 pt. Arrack
1 pt. red French wine

Pour the strained juice of two large oranges over loaf-sugar. Add a little of the out-side peel cut in very thin slices. Pour over it one quart of boiling water, one pint of Arrack and a pint of hot red French Wine. Stir together. This may be served when cold and will improve with age.

CHRISTMAS WASSAIL

2 qts. apple cider
4 cups orange juice
2 lemons—juice
4 sticks cinnamon (2″)

2 tbsps. whole cloves
2 tbsps. whole allspice
¼ tbsp. grated nutmeg or mace
¾ cup clover honey

Simmer above ingredients for ten minutes. Strain out spices. Serve in bowl decorated with holly or other Christmas greens.

EGG NOGG

1 doz. eggs
1 pt. bourbon
1 pt. brandy

1 qt. whipping cream
1 cup milk
1½ cups sugar

Beat egg yolks and sugar until stiff; beat in whiskey slowly until blended; stir in stiffly beaten cream; fold in stiffly beaten egg whites; thin mixture with milk and allow to ripen overnight. Do not drink until it has ripened at least overnight in refrigerator. Approximately 24 cups.

FRUIT PUNCH

2 cups strong tea	2 cups sugar
Juice of 5 oranges	1 cup raspberry or strawberry syrup
Juice of 5 lemons	1 qt. sparkling water
1 small can grated pineapple	1 cup candied cherries

Make syrup of 1 cup water and 2 cups sugar boiled 10 minutes. Add tea, fruit juice, orange juice, lemon juice and pineapple. Cool the mixture, strain, and add enough water to make 6 qts. of liquid. Pour over large pieces of ice in punch bowl, add cherries and just before serving, stir in sparkling water.

LIME PUNCH

2 qts. of lime sherbet
(Lime ice might be used)
4 large bottles Ginger Ale

Pour Ginger ale over lime sherbet, mix slight and serve. A delicious hot weather drink.

RHUBARB PUNCH

4 cups rhubarb, cut in small pieces	1/2 large can frozen undiluted orange juice
4 cups water	2/3 cup lemon juice
1 cup white sugar	1/4 tsp. salt
1/2 cup brown sugar	1 qt. gingerale

Combine rhubarb and water in sauce pan and cook until soft enough to put through a food mill or strainer.

Return to sauce pan, add sugars, heat, stirring constantly until sugar content is dissolved.

Add juices and salt, place in electric blender or mixer for 3 minutes. Add gingerale just before serving.

TEA PUNCH

Mix together	1 pint ice cold water
1 qt. tea	1/2 cup orange juice
1/2 cup lemon juice	2 cups or more sugar

Add 1 pint gingerale just before serving. Makes 5 pints.

BREADS

PLANTATION SPOONBREAD

1 cup cornmeal
1-1/3 cups boiling water
1-1/3 cups Fresh milk
3 whole eggs

1 tbsp. baking powder
4 tbsp. butter
1-1/3 tsp. sugar
1½ tsp. salt

Mix sugar and salt with cornmeal and blend
well. Pour boiling water over meal,
Stirring constantly. Let stand until cool.
Beat eggs until light, add eggs and baking powder
to mixture. Add milk and pour mixture into
2-quart buttered pan or baking dish.
Place in shallow pan of hot water in 350 degree
oven. Bake about 35 minutes.

Yield: 8 Servings

HEALTHY PUMPKIN-OAT BRAN MUFFINS

1 1/2 cups unprocessed oat bran
1/2 cup firmly packed brown sugar
dash cinnamon
1/2 cup all-purpose flour
pinch nutmeg
2 tsp. baking powder
1 tsp. pumpkin pie spice

1/4 tsp. salt
1 cup cooked, mashed
   pumpkin
1/2 cup low fat milk
2 egg whites, beaten
2 tbsp. vegetable oil

Combine the first 8 ingredients in a large bowl and stir well. Make a well in the center of the mixture. Combine pumpkin and next 3 ingredients and stir well. Add dry ingredients, stirring until moistened. Spoon into greased muffin pan (sprayed with vegetable oil) until cups are 3/4 full. Bake at 425 degrees for 20 minutes. Remove from pans immediately and serve warm. Makes 1 dozen muffins.

BEATEN BISCUITS

4 cups flour
2 tsps. sugar
1/2 tsp. baking powder
1/4 tsp. cream of tartar

1 rounded teaspoon salt
1/2 cup shortening, ice cold
About 1 cup ice cold water

Cut lard into dry ingredients adding ice water to make a dry dough. Beat with a hatchet about fifteen minutes until a piece of dough pulled off with a snap. Flatten dough and fold over as you beat. Roll out to 1/4 inch thickness and cut into biscuits, marking the top with 3 fork prints. Bake at 425 degrees for 10 minutes, reduce to 400 degrees for 25 minutes. Do not bake too long.

BISCUIT MIX

8 cups flour
2 tsps. salt

3 tbsps. baking powder
¾ cup shortening

Sift dry ingredients. Cut in shortening. Store until ready to use by adding sweetmilk. (½ cup to each cup of mix)

BREADS

APPLESAUCE NUT BREAD

2 cups flour sifted
3/4 cup sugar
1 tsp. baking powder
1 tsp. salt
1/2 tsp. soda

1/2 tsp. nutmeg
1 cup nuts
1 egg beaten
1 cup applesauce

Add all ingredients and stir just enough to moisten. Bake one hour in slow oven.

BANANA MUFFINS

5 lg. ripe bananas, mashed
1 egg
1/2 tsp. salt
1 cup sugar
1 teaspoon soda

1/4 cup butter, softened
1 tsp. baking powder
1 cup pecans, chopped
1 1/2 cups flour

Preheat oven to 375 degrees. Mix all of the ingredient adding the flour last. Pour into greased muffin cups and bake 15-20 minutes or until golden brown. Yield 2 dozen large muffins

APRICOT BREAD

Soak 1/2 cup dried apricots and 1/2
  cup dried raisins for 1/2 hour.
Sift together:
2 cups flour
1 tsp. soda
1/2 cup sugar
1/2 tsp. salt

2 tsps. baking powder
1 egg
2 tbsps. butter (creamed)
1 tsp. vanilla
1/2 cup walnut meats
Juice of one orange in cup (fill cup
  with boiling water)

Drain water from raisins and apricots, and put them through meat chopper. Add orange juice and water. Then add beaten egg and vanilla to creamed butter. Add sifted dry ingredients and nut meats. Bake in loaf pan for one hour at 350°F.

BATTER BREAD

1 cup cooked hominy sieved	1 tsp. sugar
1½ cups corn meal	1 tsp. baking powder
1 egg	1 tbsp. shortening
1 tsp. salt	2 cups milk

Mix everything except shortening. Batter will be thin as custard. Heat shortening in metal pan until it smokes. Pour in batter and bake at 350°F for one hour.

BLANDFIELD BATTER BREAD

1 cup white corn meal	1 scant tsp. of baking powder
4 eggs beaten separately	1 qt. of sweet milk
1 tsp. of salt	Butter the size of an egg

Sift dry ingredients. Scald milk and pour over dry ingredients. Add beaten yolks of eggs and last stir in the whites. Pour into buttered baking dish with melted butter in the dish. Stir thoroughly twice while baking.

BLUEBERRY BREAKFAST CAKE

2-3 tbsps. shortening	)
1 cup sugar	) Cream together
1 egg unbeaten	) Add
2 cups flour	)
1 tsp. baking powder	) Sift together and add
½ tsp. salt	)
1 cup milk	) Add
2 cups blueberries	)

Bake 30 minutes at 350°F in brownie tin. (9 in. square) Delicious hot bread, especially for luncheon or supper.

OLD FASHIONED BUCKWHEAT CAKES

2/3 cup buckwheat flour	1 cup warm water
1/3 cup wheat flour	½ yeast cake
½ tsp. salt	Sugar to taste
1 tbsp. syrup	

Cover the bowl and let rise all night and bake in morning. Do not stir the dough.

BREADS

CHEESE BISCUITS

½ stick butter	1 tsp. baking powder
2 cups grated sharp cheese	1 tsp. salt
1 cup flour	Dash red pepper

Bake in 350°F oven for 15 to 20 minutes. Watch carefully as they burn quickly.

BLUEBERRY MUFFINS

2 cups flour	1 egg
3 tsp. baking powder	4 tbsp. melted butter
3 tbsp. sugar	1 cup milk
1/2 tsp. salt	1 cup fresh blueberries

Preheat oven to 400. Sift flour and reserve 1/4 cup to dredge berries. Mix and sift dry ingredients. Beat egg lightly and add butter and milk. Add to dry mixture and stir enough to moisten the dry ingredients. Dredge blueberries in reserve flour and carefully stir into batter. Fill well-greased muffin cups and bake 15-20 minutes. Yields 12-15 muffins.

CHEESE ROLLS

1 pkg. yeast, compressed or dry	1 cup shredded cheese
¼ cup lukewarm water	2 tbsps. finely chopped onion
1 cup milk	1 egg
2 tbsps. sugar	3¼ cups sifted enriched flour
1 tsp. salt	(approximately)
¼ cup shortening	Caraway or poppy seeds, if desired.

Soften yeast in water. Scald milk. Add sugar, salt, shortening, shredded cheese and onion. Cool to lukewarm. Add 1 cup flour and beat well. Add softened yeast and egg and beat well. Add remaining flour to make a thick batter. Beat thoroughly until smooth. Cover and let rise in warm place until doubled (about 1 hour). When light, stir down. Drop by spoonfuls into greased muffins pans. Brush with milk and sprinkle with caraway or poppy seed. Let rise until doubled (about 45 minutes). Bake in moderate oven (375°F) about 25 minutes. Makes 18 puffs.

OLIVE BREAD

1 package dry yeast
1/2 c. warm water
2 tsp. sugar
1 1/2 c. warm milk
1/2 c. cornmeal

1 (6 oz.) can sliced ripe olives, drained
2 tbsp. olive oil
2 c. whole wheat flour
2 to 2 1/2 c. unbleached flour
1 1/2 tsp. salt

Combine yeast, warm water, and sugar in a 1-cup measuring cup and let stand for 5 minutes. Combine yeast mixture, milk, cornmeal, salt, ripe olives, olive oil, and whole wheat flour in a large bowl. Stir in one cup unbleached flour. Gradually stir in enough remaining unbleached flour to make a firm dough.

Turn dough out onto a lightly floured surface and knead until smooth (about 3 to 4 minutes). Place dough in a well-greased bowl, turning once to grease top. Cover and let rise in a warm place, free from drafts for 1 hour or until dough is double. Punch dough down and divide it in half. Shape each portion into a 6-inch ball and place on a lightly greased baking sheet. Cover and let rise in a warm place for 30 minutes or until doubled in bulk.

Bake in preheated oven at 350 degrees for 35 to 40 minutes or until loaves sound hollow when tapped. Cool before cutting.

CORN BREAD

1 egg—well beaten
1/2 cup sugar
1 tsp. salt
1 cup sour or buttermilk

1 tsp. soda
2 tbsps. melted shortening
1 cup flour
1 cup corn meal

Beat egg, add sugar. Pour in milk to which soda has been added. Add dry ingredients, beat well, add shortening. Pour into shallow pan. Bake in hot oven 400°F for approximately 25 minutes. Serve warm with butter or with creamed chicken or any creamed meat.

CORN PANCAKES

1 cup grated raw corn
1 egg, beaten whole
1 tbsp. milk

Flour to hold together
1/4 tsp. salt
1 tbsp. melted butter

Beat egg well, add corn slowly. Add salt and melted butter. Stir in milk and enough flour to hold together. Drop on griddle and cook like pancakes. Perfect with steak gravy.

BREADS

CORN MEAL WAFFLES

1¾ cups meal	1 tsp. salt
¼ cup flour	2 tsps. baking powder
2 eggs	1/3 cup cooking oil or melted fat
¼ tsp. soda	1¼ to 1½ cups buttermilk

Sift salt and meal together. Beat eggs; add buttermilk and shortening. Combine with sifted meal and salt. Sift flour, soda, and baking powder together and add to other mixture. Cook immediately.

CRACKLING BREAD

1 cup cracklings, diced	¼ tsp. salt
2 cups corn meal	½ tsp. soda
1 cup sour milk or buttermilk	

Cracklings are the pieces of meat remaining after the lard has been rendered from the pork. Mix and sift together the dry ingredients. Add the milk, stir in cracklings. Form into oblong cakes and place on greased baking pan. Bake in hot oven 450°F for 30 minutes.

DATE NUT LOAF

1 lb. dates	4 eggs
1 cup flour	2 tsps. baking powder
1 cup white sugar	½ tsp. salt
1 lb. walnut and Brazil nut meats	1 tsp. vanilla

Beat egg yolks and whites separately. Over nuts and dates, sift flour, salt and baking powder. Cream sugar in yolks. Into this, fold well-floured dates and nuts. Stir in whites and vanilla. Pour in greased loaf pan and bake 1 hour at 350°F.

DILLY BREAD

1 pkg. dry or one cake compressed yeast
1/4 cup warm water
1 cup creamed cottage cheese, heated to lukewarm
2 tbsps. sugar
1 tbsp. instant minced onion

1 tbsp. butter
2 tsps. dill seed
1 tsp. salt
1/2 tsp. soda
1 unbeaten egg
2 1/4 to 2 1/2 cups all-purpose flour

Soften yeast in water. Combine in mixing bowl cottage cheese, sugar, onion, butter, dill seed, salt, soda, egg and softened yeast. Add flour to form a stiff dough, beating well after each addition. Cover. Let rise in warm place until light and doubled in size, 50-60 minutes. Stir down dough. Turn into well-greased eight inch round casserole (1 1/2 to 2 quarts). Let rise in warm place until light, 30-40 minutes. Bake at 350°F for 40-50 minutes until golden brown. Brush with soft butter and sprinkle with salt. Make one loaf.

ENGLISH TEACAKES

1 1/4 qts. flour (5 cups)
1/2 cup shortening, rubbed in
1/2 cup sugar
2 cups scalded milk (let cool)

1 yeastcake blended in a little warm water
1/2 tsp. salt
1 beaten egg

Knead well. After raising, knead on floured board and form into buns, put on baking sheet and let raise for about an hour. Bake about 25 minutes in moderate oven.

HUSH PUPPIES

1 egg
1 cup corn meal
1 tbsp. flour
1/2 tsp. salt

1 1/2 tsp. baking powder
1/4 tsp. black pepper
1 large onion
1/2 to 3/4 cup sweet milk

Sift together corn meal, flour, salt, baking powder, and pepper. Add 1 large mild onion, peeled and chopped fine and 1 egg. Mix and beat well, then add a little at a time about 1/2 to 3/4 cup sweet milk. Beat the batter well until it is smooth, and drop by tablespoons from side of spoon into at least 2 inches of hot fat 375°F and fry until golden brown. Dip the hush puppies out with a perforated spoon, let drain a moment and then serve sizzling hot.

BREADS

HUSH PUPPIES

1/2 cup sifted flour	*2 tsps. baking powder
1 1/2 cups corn meal	*3/4 tsp. salt
1 egg, beaten	6 tbsps. minced onion
3/4 cup sweet milk	

*If self-rising corn meal and flour are used, omit salt and baking powder.

Sift together the dry ingredients. Add onion, beaten egg and milk. Stir lightly to moisten well. Drop a scant teaspoon of batter for each hush puppy into hot deep fat (365°F). Cook until brown. When done they will float. Drain on absorbent paper.

LUNCH ROLLS

Scald 1 1/4 cups milk	When cool add
Add	1 yeast cake dissolved in warm water
2 tsp. shortening	1 egg beaten light
1 tsp. sugar	Flour to make dough soft
1 tsp. salt	

Knead well, keeping dough soft, let rise about 2 hours. Roll out, making turnovers or small rolls. Let rise for about 45 min. and bake in a hot oven.

CRANBERRY BREAD

2 c. flour	1 c. fresh or frozen cranberries, chopped
3/4 c. sugar	1 egg, beaten
1 tsp. salt	1 1/2 tsp. baking powder
1/2 tsp. soda	3/4 cup orange juice
1/2 c. chopped nuts	2 tbsp. salad oil

Preheat oven to 350. Sift dry ingredients together. Stir in nuts and cranberries. Add remaining ingredients and mix until moistened. Bake in greased, floured loaf pan for 50 minutes or until golden brown.

DUMPLINGS FOR STEW

1 cup flour
2 tsps. baking powder

1/2 tsp. salt
1/3 cup milk

Sift dry ingredients together. Add liquid gradually, stirring with a knife. Drop by spoonful on top of stew. Cover and cook 12 minutes without lifting cover. Serves 6.

HUSH PUPPIES

1 lb. fine corn meal
1 egg
1 tbsp. salt

1 tbsp. sugar
Pinch soda
1 cup buttermilk

Stir, adding water, to thick consistency. Drop in deep fat. (preferably peanut oil). Cook in temperature of 375°F.

MADISON CAKES

2 medium Irish potatoes
1¼ cups boiling water
Butter or lard size of an egg
2 tsps. salt
2 tsps. sugar

1 yeast cake
2 eggs
1½ qts. flour (½ of flour may be
    whole wheat)

Cook potatoes in boiling water. Mash thoroughly when done. Add enough cold water to potato water to make a cupful, let cool until lukewarm. Add yeast cake. To mashed potatoes add butter, salt, sugar & eggs, beating until there are no lumps. Add dissolved yeast cake, then flour. Knead until dough feels smooth and velvety, adding more flour as necessary. Put in greased crock & let rise 4 or 5 hrs. until light. Then roll inch thick & cut out or pinch off & make into rolls. Let rise until light. Bake 20 min. Put far apart in pan.

MARYLAND CREAM WAFFLES

2 eggs
1¾ cup milk
2 tsps. sugar
½ tsp. salt

2 cups flour
4 tsps. baking powder
½ cup melted butter

Beat eggs in bowl, add milk, then sift in dry ingredients. Add melted butter and beat well.

52

BREADS

NUT BREAD

2 eggs
2 cups sweet milk
1 cup sugar
4 cups flour

4 tsps. baking powder
1/2 tsp. salt
1/2 to 1 cup nuts

Pour into well greased pan and let rise 15 or 20 min. Bake in slow oven ¾-1 hour. Makes 2 loaves.

OATMEAL BREAD

Pour 2 cups hot water over 1 cup
   Quaker oats. Let stand until soft.
   Then mix with
1/2 tbsp. salt
Butter the size of egg

1/2 cup molasses
1/3 cup sugar
2 yeast cakes in 1/3 cup warm water
5 cups flour

Let rise until double in bulk. Cut down and let rise again. Knead and shape into two loaves. Bake one hour at 350°F.

OLD VIRGINIA SPOON BREAD

1 cup cornmeal
1 tbsp. shortening
1 tsp. salt
1 cup boiling water

2 cups milk
2 eggs
3 tsps. baking powder

Mix salt with cornmeal, cut in shortening; slowly pour in cup of boiling water, stirring as you pour in; beat the eggs in the milk to blend well and stir in; then add baking powder and blend all ingredients well. Grease casserole generously and pour in ingredients. Cook in medium oven 350°F and bake 30 minutes or until brown on top. While baking it should be stirred two or three times before ingredients congeal. Serve hot from casserole. Serves 4 to 6.

ORANGE TEA BISCUITS

2 cups flour	4 tsps. butter
4 tsps. baking powder	¾ cup of milk
½ tsp. salt	A few lumps of loaf sugar
1 tsp. grated orange rind	Orange juice

Sift flour before measuring. Sift dry ingredients together, add grated rind, cut in shortening, add milk, roll and cut, put in well greased pans. Dip half a sugar lump in orange juice and press down in middle of each biscuit. Bake in hot oven 10 minutes.

POPOVERS

1 cup sifted enriched flour	1 cup milk
½ tsp. salt	1 tbsp. melted shortening
2 eggs, beaten	

Sift together flour and salt. Combine eggs and milk. Add to flour mixture and beat to a smooth batter. Add shortening. Beat 3 minutes with rotary beater. Pour into well greased glass custard cups or heated iron muffin pans, filling ½ full. Bake in hot oven (425°F) 35 to 40 minutes. Makes 6 large popovers.

MUFFINS

2 cups flour	2 tbsps. melted fat
1 tbsp. baking powder	1 cup milk
½ tsp. salt	2 tsps. sugar (optional)
2 eggs	

Melt fat in muffin tins. Sift dry ingredients. Mix in other ingredients quickly. Have pans and oven hot (425°F). Bake 10 to 15 minutes. Do not beat muffin batter; beating will produce tunnels.

POTATO ROLLS

1½ cups lukewarm water	2/3 cup shortening
1 pkg. dry yeast	2 eggs
1/3 cup sugar	1 cup lukewarm mashed potatoes
1½ tsp. salt	7½ cups flour

Mix flour with hands until dough is easily handled. Knead, place in greased bowl. Punch down (1½ to 2 hours). Shape in 2 inch balls, let rise until double in bulk. Bake at 400°F for 12 to 15 minutes.

BREADS

SAGE BISCUITS

2 cups flour
1/2 tsp. salt
1 tsp. baking powder
1/2 tsp. soda

1/2 tsp. sage
3 tbsps. shortening
3/4 to 1 cup buttermilk

Sift flour; measure; add salt, baking powder, and soda. Sift together. Add sage; cut in shortening, and add buttermilk. Mix until blended. Knead lightly. Roll 3/8" thick. Cut out with biscuit cutter. Bake 12-15 minutes in 475°F oven.

HERBED BISCUITS

2 cups all purpose flour
1/2 tsp. baking powder
1/4 tsp. dried thyme, crushed
1/4 tsp. dried rosemary, crushed
1/4 tsp. dried basil, crushed

1 tbsp. baking powder
1/4 tsp. salt
1/4 cup butter
3/4 cup low fat buttermilk

Combine the first 7 ingredients in a large bowl and cut in butter with a pastry blender until mixture is pea size crumbs. Add buttermilk, stirring with a fork just until dry ingredients are moistened. Turn dough out onto a lightly floured surface and knead lightly half a dozen times. Roll dough to 1/2 inch thickness and cut with a 2 inch round cutter. Place biscuits on an ungreased cookie sheet, and bake at 400 degrees for 10 to 12 minutes. Serve warm. Makes 12 biscuits.

"...MAN SHALL NOT LIVE BY BREAD ALONE..."
MATTHEW 4:4

ROLLS

1 cup hot water
1 tsp. salt
6 tbsp. shortening
1 yeast cake

¼ cup granulated sugar
2 tbsps. lukewarm water
1 egg well beaten
3¾ cup sifted flour

Combine hot water, salt, shortening and sugar in large bowl—cool to lukewarm, add yeast softened in lukewarm water. Add egg, half the flour and beat well. Stir in more of the flour, enough to make the dough easily handled. Grease top of dough and store in refrigerator. Let rise about 1½ hours before cooking. Bake in hot oven 425°F for 12 to 15 minutes.

RUSKS

1 fresh yeast cake
1 cup scalded milk
2 cups flour
½ cup shortening
2 well beaten eggs

Flavoring as desired
2 cups or enough flour to make stiff
    dough
1 cup sugar

Make sponge using all ingredients except sugar and let rise. After sponge has risen add sugar. Let rise until double in bulk and then form into biscuit shapes and let rise again. Mix ½ cup sugar with 1 tbsp. ground ginger and moisten with water and spread on top of each rusk. Bake slowly.

SALLY LUNN

2 tbsps. sugar
1 tsp. salt
3 eggs beaten separately
1 cup milk, warmed

¾ cup butter—melted
5 cups flour
1 yeast cake dissolved in 1 cup
    water

Put yeast in small bowl and pour warm water over it, add sugar and salt and let stand while you are getting other things together. Melt butter and set aside. Separate eggs and beat yolks in large bowl. Add warm milk and yeast. Add flour a little at a time and beat while adding. Add beaten whites, melted butter and beat together until it blisters. Let rise in a warm place until twice its size, about 1½ or 2 hours. Beat again and turn into well greased cake mold or loaf pans. Let rise again until it has doubled its size. Cook in oven at 375°F until brown, ½ to ¾ hour, Turn it out and serve while hot.

BREADS

TAVERN SWEET POTATO MUFFINS

1/2 cup sugar	4 tbsp. butter
2/3 cup sweet potato cooked and drained	1 egg
	3/4 cup all-purpose flour
2 tsp. baking powder	1/2 tsp. salt
1/2 tsp. cinnamon	1/4 tsp. nutmeg
1/2 cup milk	1/4 cup pecans, chopped
	1/4 cup raisins, chopped

Grease muffin tins and preheat oven to 400 degrees. Puree the sweet potatoes in a blender. Cream the butter and sugar. Beat in eggs and sweet potatoes. Sift the flour with the other dry ingredients. Add this dry mixture to the butter mixture. Mix in milk and nuts and raisins, just until blended. Spoon into the greased muffin tins, filling each tin completely. A little cinnamon-sugar may be sprinkled on top of each muffin. Bake at 400 degrees for 25 minutes.

SPOON BREAD

1 cup corn meal	4 eggs
1/2 tsp. salt	1 cup milk
2 tbsps. butter	

Stir corn meal into one pint of boiling water, which contains one half teaspoon of salt. Stir one minute, remove from fire and add butter. Beat well, add four beaten eggs and beat in cold milk. Beat again and pour into hot buttered baking dish. Bake 25 minutes in hot oven and serve from baking dish.

SHORT BREAD

4 ozs. flour
1 oz. sugar
2½ ozs. butter

Method—Sift flour, rub in butter, add sugar and knead well until blended. Roll out ¼ inch thick, cut into strips or pieces. Put in a buttered tin. Cook in moderate oven for 20 or 30 minutes. Allow to cool before taking from oven.

SOUTHERN SPOON BREAD

2 cups boiling water
1 cup white cornmeal
1 tbsp. Wesson oil or butter
1 tsp. salt
2 tsps. baking powder
2 eggs
2 cups milk

Pour boiling water over meal, stirring constantly, and boil 5 minutes. Remove from stove, add Wesson oil or butter, salt and milk. Mix well. Beat eggs light, add to mixture, sift in baking powder, mix well, and pour into greased baking dish and bake one-half hour in a moderate oven (350°F). Serve from dish in which it was baked while piping hot.

SWEDISH TIMBALES

¾ cup bread flour
½ tsp. salt
1 tsp. sugar
½ cup milk
1 egg
1 tsp. oil

Sift dry ingredients. Add milk gradually, then add beaten egg and oil. Put mixture in a cup. Heat timbale iron in deep fat until fat is hot enough to brown a cube of bread in 1 min. When hot, dip iron three-fourths into batter, then into fat until brown. Drain on brown paper.

VIRGINIA CORN MUFFINS

2 cups corn meal
2 tsps. baking powder
½ tsp. soda
½ tsp. salt
1 tsp. sugar
2 eggs
¼ cup melted fat
2 cups buttermilk (more if needed)

Sift meal with dry ingredients. Add milk, eggs, and fat, and beat with rotary egg beater. Have greased muffin tins hot. Add batter to hot tins and bake in hot oven 450°F about 25 minutes.

BREADS

VIRGINIA HAM BISCUITS

2 cups flour	2 tbsps. shortening
4 tsps. baking powder	¾ cup milk
Pinch salt	¼ cup ground Virginia Ham

Sift flour and baking powder, mix with salt and ham, cut in shortening with a knife until all is consistency of meal, add milk, handle as little as possible. Pat out with hands or roll on floured board, cut out, and bake in hot oven till brown.

WAFFLES

2 cups flour	½ tsp. salt
1½ cups milk	2 eggs (yellows and whites beaten separately)
2 tbsps. sugar	6 tbsps. melted butter or oil
3 tsps. baking powder	

Sift flour, add dry ingredients. Beat yellows of eggs and add milk to them. Mix alternately with dry ingredients. Stir in oil or butter. Beat egg whites stiff and add last to mixture.

YORKSHIRE PUDDING

1 cup flour	¼ tsp. salt
1 cup milk	Beef drippings
2 eggs	

Sift flour and salt together. Beat eggs well and add to flour mixing well. Slowly add the milk and beat with egg beater for 2 minutes. Heat thoroughly an oblong pan and then grease well with the beef drippings. Pour in the batter about ½ inch deep. Bake in a hot oven (450°F) for 20 minutes. Reduce the heat to moderately hot (400°F) and bake 20 minutes longer. Serve with roast beef and gravy.

VIRGINIA HAM MUFFINS

1 cup flour	1/2 tsp. sugar
3 tsps. baking powder	2/3 cup milk
Pinch salt	1 egg
3/4 cup ground Virginia Ham	1 tbsp. melted butter

Sift dry ingredients, add ham, mix in well beaten egg and shortening. Drop one spoonful of batter into each greased muffin tin. Bake in hot oven 20 to 30 minutes.

VIRGINIA WAFFLES

1¾ cups flour	3 level tsps. baking powder
2/3 cup ground Virginia Ham	1/8 tsp. salt
1¼ cups milk	1 tbsp. melted butter
2 eggs	

Sift dry ingredients, add ham, milk and beaten yolks of egg, and butter. Beat well and last fold in stiffly whipped white of eggs. Fry in waffle iron. Serve plain with butter or with syrup.

WAFFLES

2 cups of flour	2 cups of sweet milk
6 tsps. baking powder	2 eggs
1/2 tsp. salt	6 tbsps. of melted butter
1 tsp. sugar	

Sift thoroughly the flour, salt, sugar and baking powder. Add slowly the milk and well-beaten eggs, stirring all to a smooth paste. If the mixture does not come perfectly smooth, it may be beaten with a rotary egg beater.

"Bread is still the world's staff
of life. In 6000 years man has
never lost his taste for it."

MEATS

HOW TO COOK AN
OLD VIRGINIA HAM

Select a three to five year old ham weighing
twelve to eighteen pounds. Trim and wash
carefully and soak overnight. Change water and add
one cup of apple vinegar and one cup of
brown sugar. Cover with water. Boil very slowly
five to six hours, or until end bone is loose. Leave
the ham in the water in which it was cooked
until the water is cold then skin. Put ham in
baking pan and bake to a nice brown.

APPLE STUFFING

1/4 lb. salt pork
1/4 cup chopped onion
2 cups diced tart apple

1/4 cup firmly packed brown sugar
2 cups soft bread crumbs
Few grains salt

Fry salt pork until crisp. Add onion; saute. Add apples and sugar; cook until tender. Add crumbs and salt. Mix well. Makes enough to stuff 6 lb. boned pork shoulder.

APRICOT STUFFING

1/2 lb. dried apricots
2 cups bread crumbs
1/4 cup cracker crumbs
1 1/2 tsps. salt

1/4 tsp. paprika
4 tbsps. chopped celery
1 tbsp. minced parsley
4 tbsps. butter, melted

Wash apricots, cover with cold water and cook until tender. Drain and chop the apricots fine. Combine crumbs with seasonings, celery and parsley. Stir in melted fat, then add chopped apricots. Mix well. This will fill a 4-5 pound fowl.

ARMENIAN SHISH-KABOB

4 lbs. boneless lamb, cut into 1 1/2"
   cubes
1/2 cup olive oil
1 minced garlic clove
1/2 cup chopped pimento-stuffed
   olives
1 tsp. salt
1/2 tsp. ground black pepper

1/2 tsp. dill seed
1 tsp. grated lemon rind
3 tbsps. lemon juice
3 large green peppers, cut in half and
   seeded
6 small, peeled onions
6 large mushrooms
3 large, firm tomatoes, cut in half

Trim excess fat from lamb; place meat in a shallow pan. Combine olive oil, garlic, olives, salt, pepper, dill seed, lemon rind and juice. Pour over meat in pan and refrigerate for at least 12 hours, turning occasionally so that marinade penetrates all meat surfaces. Three quarters of an hour before serving, turn on broiler. Thread meat on a long skewer and broil for 20 to 25 minutes 5 inches from heat, turning occasionally to brown all sides. Meanwhile, thread green pepper halves and onions on another skewer. Broil the last 10 minutes that the meat cooks. Arrange mushrooms and tomato halves on a third skewer and broil the last 5 minutes of cooking time. Baste foods on all skewers occasionally with marinade from meat. Remove foods to serving platter and serve with Rice Pilaf. Makes 6 servings.

MEATS

BAKED PORK CHOPS WITH RICE

4 pork chops	1/4 cup uncooked rice
6 medium onions (chopped)	1 can tomato soup
1 tsp. salt	1 can water

Place chops on bottom of casserole, cover with onions and sprinkle with salt. Pour uncooked rice over onions and chops, add tomato soup thinned with water. Bake covered for 1½ hours at 350°F.

BARBECUE SAUCE

1/2 cup salad oil	3 tbsps. sugar
3/4 cup chopped onion	3 tbsps. Worcestershire sauce
3/4 cup ketchup	2 tbsps. prepared mustard
3/4 cup water	2 tsps. salt
1/3 cup lemon juice	1/2 tsp. pepper

Cook onion until soft in hot oil. Add remaining ingredients. Simmer slowly 30 minutes. Baste frequently on ribs or chicken, or pour over meat and bake.

BARBECUED SPARE RIBS

1. Cut 3 to 4 lb. ribs into servings. Salt.
2. Slice 2 medium onions.
3. Blend:

2 tbsps. vinegar	Pinch red pepper
2 tsps. salt	1/2 tsp. paprika
1 tbsp. Worcestershire	1/2 tsp. chili powder
2 tsps. brown sugar	1/4 tsp. black pepper
3/4 cup catsup	3/4 cup water

Arrange 1, 2, and 3 in layers in roasting pan. Bake, covered 90 minutes at 350°F. Remove cover. Bake 20 minutes longer at 375°F.

BARBECUED VENISON

1 cup catsup	1/4 cup vinegar
1 tbsp. salt	1 onion, sliced thin
2 tbsps. Worcestershire sauce	1/8 tsp. of allspice
1 tbsp. butter	3 slices of lemon

Mix ingredients and bring to a boil. Simmer, stirring occasionally, for 10 minutes. Pour over 3 pounds of venison which has been sauteed in hot fat to brown. Roast in a moderate oven (350°F) for 1 to 2 hours, turning occasionally.

WILLIAMSBURG MEAT LOAF

1 lb. round steak and	
1/4 lb. salt pork ground together	2 heaping tsp. salt
2 cups bread crumbs	Dash of pepper and celery salt
1 1/2 cups water	1 egg

Mix all together and bake at 375 degrees about an hour in a well greased pan.

BARBECUED PORK LOIN

1 boneless pork loin breast, trimmed to about 2 to 2 1/2 lbs.

3/4 cup catsup	3/4 cup onion, finely chopped
1 clove garlic, minced	1 tbsp. honey
1 1/2 tsp. unsweetened cocoa	1 1/2 tsp. brown sugar
2 1/4 teaspoon lemon juice	1 1/2 teaspoons liquid smoke
1/4 teaspoon pepper	dash of mace

Cut roast down the center length-wise, cutting to within 1/2 inch of the other side. Pull roast open and place in a shallow dish. Combine catsup and next 9 ingredients stirring well. Spread half of marinade mixture over both sides of roast, reserving remaining marinade. Cover roast, and refrigerate overnight or at least 8 hours. Cover and refrigerate reserve mixture.

Coat grill rack with cooking spray and get coals hot. Remove roast from marinade, discarding marinade. Place roast on rack, and cook turning once, 20 minutes or until meat is cooked well. Remove from grill and slice thinly. Warm reserved marinade in a heavy saucepan. Pour over sliced pork.

MEATS

BEEF POTPIE

2 lb. boneless chuck	1/2 tsp. paprika
1 onion	1/4 tsp. pepper
1 clove garlic	1 tsp. Worcestershire sauce
1 bay leaf	6 carrots
1 tbsp. salt	6 small potatoes
1 tsp. sugar	6 small onions

Cut beef into 1 inch cubes. In dutch oven, brown meat on all sides in small amount of hot fat. Take plenty of time for browning. Slice onion and add garlic, bay leaf, salt, sugar, paprika, pepper and Worcestershire sauce. Add 3 cups water. Cook at a gentle bubble—boiling toughens meat. Cover pan and simmer lazily 1½ hours, stir occasionally to prevent sticking. Remove bay leaf and garlic. Add carrots cut in 2 inch lengths, potatoes cut in halves and onions, cook 30 minutes longer. Add cup frozen peas; continue cooking 10 minutes more. Serves 6 to 8.

BONELESS COUNTRY FRIED CHICKEN
(With Supreme Sauce)

Boil 5 lb. chicken until tender with onion, celery, carrot, salt and pepper. When cooked remove chicken from bones and break down to portion size. Roll chicken in flour. Dip chicken in egg wash consisting of:

2 eggs	Pinch of salt
1 pt. milk	Pinch of pepper

Roll in cracker crumbs. Fry in deep fat at 365°F for 3 minutes.

Supreme sauce

2 cups chicken stock, bring to boil. Thicken with following: Melt 2 tbsp. oleo and add 2 tbsp. flour. Cook until thickened. Season with salt and pepper. Pour over fried chicken. Serves four.

Cook until thickened. Season with salt and pepper. Pour over fried chicken. Serves four.

BEEF STEW

3 lbs. stew beef, cut into 1 inch cubes	1½ cups bouillon
4 tbsps. butter or oleo	3 tbsps. flour
½ lb. mushrooms	1 cup red wine (claret or burgundy—
1 large can boiled onions	not a sweet wine)
1 tsp. bouillon paste	Herbs to taste — parsley, bay leaf,
1 tsp. tomato paste	pepper, salt, thyme, etc..

Brown beef in butter. Remove from pan. Brown mushrooms and onions. Add tomato paste, bouillon paste, flour and stir in. Add bouillon slowly. When thickened, add wine. Add herbs. Add beef. Cook 1 to 2 hours, covered, slowly.

CHICKEN CACCIATORE

4 lbs. disjointed chicken	1 No. 2 can tomatoes
½ cup flour	1 green pepper
1/3 cup olive oil	1 can tomato paste
1 garlic clove	¼ lb. mushrooms
2 medium onions	Salt and pepper

Dredge chicken in flour and brown in hot fat. Add minced garlic, chopped onions, diced green pepper, with tomatoes, tomato paste and mushrooms. Salt and pepper to taste. Simmer about one hour or until the chicken is tender. Serves 6.

CHICKEN WITH RICE PIE

Fat hen, weighing 4 or 5 pounds	½ tsp. thyme
3 qts. of salted water	1 cup of rice
Parsley	2 well beaten eggs
½ onion	

Cook the hen in the salted water to which may be added the herbs and the onion as flavor. Simmer till done, but still firm. Remove the hen from the stock, stuff it with a well seasoned dressing and bake it in a 400°F oven until brown, basting with some of the stock which should be around it in the pan.

In the stock in which the hen has simmered, cook the rice, simmering it it about 25 minutes in a covered pan. Add the well beaten eggs to the rice. Place the roasted hen on a serving platter and surround it with the rice, adding parsley as a decorative touch, if desired. If preferred, the rice may be turned out into a baking dish and baked till firm and brown, and served with the hen.

MEATS

CHICKEN A LA BOURGOISE

1 lb. beef	1 pinch thyme
1 lb. veal bones	4 sprigs parsley
1 carrot	1 small can tomatoes
1 Bermuda onion	1 stalk celery
1 tbsp. salt	1 small bay leaf

Spread out in a flat pan beef and veal bones. Add carrott and Bermuda onion (in thick slices). Brown the bone well on all sides in a moderately hot oven. Transfer all ingredients to a kettle and add 2½ qts. cold water, salt, thyme, parsley, tomatoes, celery and bay leaf.

Bring slowly to a boil, skimming when necessary. Continue cooking slowly for 4 hours, or until stock is reduced to about 2 qts. Strain through a fine sieve or cheesecloth and store in the refrigerator until ready to use for making brown sauce.

Sauce

3 tbsps. clarified butter	3 tbsps. bread flour
2 tsps. paprika	1 qt. stock

Melt the butter in a sauce pan. Add paprika and flour. Cook slowly over low flame, stirring occasionally until this roux is thoroughly blended and the color of brown wrapping paper. Moisten gradually with one quart of warm stock, bring to a boil, and cook 3 to 5 minutes, stirring occasionally. Skim off the fat and strain through a fine sieve. Add, to taste, some white wine (Chablis type).

Chicken

The chicken used is a double boneless breast, lightly sauted in butter, cut carrots, celery, green peas, and small pearl onions served in a casserole with the sauce and garnished with chopped parsley.

67

COMPANY CASSEROLE

4 cups (½ pound) noodles
1 tbsp. butter
1 lb. ground chuck
2 8-oz. cans tomato sauce
½ lb. cottage cheese

1 8-oz. package cream cheese
¼ cup dairy sour cream
1/3 cup minced scallions
1 tbsp. minced green pepper
2 tbsps. melted butter

Early in the day, cook the noodles as directed on the package; drain. Next, in a skillet saute the ground meat in butter. Stir in tomato sauce. Remove from heat. Combine cottage cheese, cream cheese, sour cream, scallions, and green pepper. In a 2-quart casserole, spread half the noodles, cover with the cheese mixture; then cover with the rest of the noodles. Pour melted butter over the noodles, then the tomato-meat sauce. Chill. About an hour before serving bake in a 350°F oven. Makes 8 servings.

CHICKEN JULIET

1 3-lb. chicken split in half
1 cup of capers
¾ stick butter
1½ tsps. salt
½ tsp. pepper

1 minced garlic clove or powder
1 cup diced mushrooms
1 cup sherry wine to be added last 5 minutes of cooking

Melt butter and mix with above ingredients except wine. Mix well. Pre-heat oven 10 minutes about 350°F or 375°F. Place chicken in baking pan skin side down. Pour ½ of mixture over it. Bake 30 minutes (longer for larger chicken), then turn over, skin side up, and pour other half of mixture over it and bake 30 minutes more. Add the cup of sherry the last 5 minutes of cooking.

CHICKEN SUPREME

Sliced cooked chicken
1 can cream of chicken soup (un-diluted)
1 tsp. lemon juice

½ tps. Worcestershire Sauce
2 tbsps. Sherry
1 bunch of broccoli or 1 package frozen broccoli

Make sauce by heating soup in a double boiler and adding the lemon juice, Worcestershire sauce and Sherry. Cook broccoli and cover with slices of chicken and the hot sauce. Sprinkle with grated cheese.

MEATS

COOKED VIRGINIA HAM, CREAMED

3 cups half-inch cubes, cooked
Virginia Ham
2 cups medium thick cream sauce
made from:

2 tbsps. butter
3 tbsps. flour
2 cups milk
1/2 tsp. salt

Melt butter in the top part of a double boiler and mix in flour to a smooth paste. Stir in milk slowly and cook until thickened. Add salt and ham. Cook over hot water until the ham is thoroughly heated. Serve on hot waffles.

COUNTRY CAPTAIN CHICKEN

3 chickens (frying size)

Cut chickens up for frying. Dip in flour to which paprika has been added. Fry in deep fat. As you take it out of the fat, steam it in a little water. Into a clean frying pan put:

1 stick oleomargarine
2 chopped garlic cloves or garlic
salt

3 small onions cut up
1 1/2 diced green pepper (large)

Cook, but do not brown. Add a little water to keep from browning. Add the following:

1 1/2 tsps. curry powder
3 tsps. mustard
Dash of red and black pepper
1 tsp. vinegar
1/2 cup chopped parsley
1 1/2 tsps. thyme

1 1/2 tbsps. Worcestershire Sauce
2 large cans of tomatoes
1 tbsp. cloves (optional)
(Best to put cloves in a small bag so
they can be removed)

Cook for a little while, adding 4 tablespoons of the grease chicken was fried in. Put in roaster. Add chicken and 1 cup of currants sprinkled on top. Put in moderate oven and cook 45 minutes with the cover on. Toast 1/2 lb. almonds without salt or grease. Cook box of rice and put in a ring on platter. Pour some of the sauce over it. Add almonds to what is left in roaster and pour this over all. Serves 8 or 10.

CREOLE STEW

In a buttered casserole, place the following ingredients:
  one layer sliced raw potatoes
  one layer sliced raw onions
  one layer partly cooked rice

Repeat each layer. Spread uncooked hamburger over top. Over all, pour one can Campbell's tomato soup and an equal amount of water. For a medium sized casserole, use about ¾ lb. hamburger. Bake 1½ hours at 375°F. This is very nutritous.

HAM LOAF

1½ lbs. lean smoked ham, ground
¾ lbs. lean fresh pork, ground
1½ cups soft bread crumbs
1½ tsps. Worcestershire sauce
⅛ tsp. pepper
1 egg
1 cup milk
Flour

Mix together meats, crumbs, seasonings, egg and milk; shape in loaf, lay in greased roaster and sprinkle with flour. Bake in moderately hot oven (375°F), about 1 hour, or until browned.

LIVER IN SOUR CREAM
(a la Gordon Block)

2 pounds calves liver sliced ½ inch thick
1 stick butter (½ for onions and ½ for liver)
1¼ tsps. salt—dash of pepper
Flour to dredge liver in
3 medium size onions
6 medium size mushrooms, sliced
1 cup sour cream

Remove skin and tough fibers from liver; place salt, pepper, flour and liver in a paper bag and shake well.

Saute onions and mushrooms in ½ stick butter until onions are brown. Pre-heat skillet to 350°F. Then add ½ stick of butter and fry liver not longer than one minute on each side. Remove liver from skillet. Use the drippings from the skillet and gradually add ¼ cup of water. stirring constantly to free lumps. Add onions, mushrooms and sour cream and allow to simmer for a few minutes. Pour this mixture over the liver, add a little lemon juice and serve.

2 pounds of chicken livers may be substituted for calves liver.

MEATS

HAM SOUFFLE

3 cups finely minced cooked Virginia Ham	1 cup milk
2 tbsps. butter	¾ tsp. salt
2 tbsps. flour	4 egg yolks, slightly beaten
	4 egg whites, beaten to stiff froth

Mix the butter and flour over moderate heat until smooth. Add milk and cook until thickened. Add salt. Stir into the egg yolks. Add ham. Fold in egg whites. Pour into a buttered casserole. Bake in slow oven 300°F until set. Serve immediately.

HAM TURNOVERS

Butter	4 eggs
2 cups ground cooked Virginia Ham	Salt and pepper

Heat a skillet and melt enough butter to cover the bottom. Warm the ham. Remove to a hot dish. Beat the eggs enough to mix the yolks and whites. Season lightly. Pour them in the skillet and cook over moderate heat until set and browned underneath. Spread the warmed ham over the egg and fold as you would an omelet. Serve on a hot platter.

LAMB STEW

2 lbs. breast of lamb (fat free), cut in 2 inch cubes	3 medium-sized carrots, quartered
2 tbsps. fat	2 tbsps. chopped parsley
10 cups hot water	1 tbsp. chopped green pepper (may omit)
Salt and pepper	8 whole black peppers
12 small white onions	½ cabbage cut up
2 potatoes, cut in eighths	1 bay leaf

Thoroughly brown meat in hot fat. Add hot water; season. Cover and simmer 1½ hours. Add vegetables; continue cooking 30 min. Serves 6-8.

VIRGINIA CHICKEN AND HAM IN MUSHROOM GRAPE SAUCE

6 boned chicken half-breast	6 slices Virginia ham
4 tbsp. butter, melted	Mushroom Grape Sauce (recipe below)

Remove chicken skin and place breast in a broiler pan and brush with butter. Broil 3 to four inches from heat for 15 minutes, turn and brush with butter.

Lower pan to 8 inches from heat, and broil 10 to 15 minutes longer. Remove from oven. Serve each half of chicken breast on a slice of ham. Top with Mushroom Grape sauce.

MUSHROOM GRAPE SAUCE

12 mushrooms	1/4 cup butter
2 tbsp lemon juice	1/4 cup all purpose flour
2 tbsp sugar	1/2 tsp. salt
2 cups seedless grapes	2 cups canned chicken broth

Saute whole mushrooms in butter, remove and set aside. Add flour and salt to butter and stir until smooth. Add chicken stock, stirring constantly. Add lemon juice and sugar. Add grapes just before serving. Garnish each ham-chicken serving with two mushrooms and spoon grape sauce over the top of each.

BEEF-CABBAGE ROLLS

1 large head cabbage	1 cup milk
1 lb. ground beef	2 tbsps. fat
2 tsps. salt	2 tbsps. brown sugar
1/4 tsp. pepper	1/2 cup hot water
1 cup cooked rice	

Soak cabbage leaves in hot water until soft. Combine meat, salt, pepper, cooked rice, milk and mix well. Place tablespoon of meat mixture into each cabbage leaf; roll leaf around meat and fasten with toothpick. Brown rolls lightly in the 2 tbsp. fat in pressure cooker. Sprinkle with brown sugar and add ½ cup hot water. Cook at 15 lbs. pressure for 10 minutes. Serve with a tomato sauce or butter. Found to be ideal for that "one hot dish" on a picnic.

MEATS

RAISIN SAUCE

1 cup brown sugar
1/3 cup grape juice
1/3 cup pineapple juice
1/2 cup crushed, drained pineapple

1/2 cup seedless raisins
3 tbsps. lemon juice
4 tbsps. vinegar
1/4 tsp. cloves

Combine all ingredients and cook 15 to 20 minutes. Serve hot or cold with ham.

RABBIT

1 rabbit
1 cup water
1/2 lb. butter

2 onions
Salt
Pepper

Melt butter; add cut up rabbit, water, onion, salt, and pepper. Cover and simmer for about 3 hours.

RAREBIT
(A Bachelor's Recipe)

1 pound rat cheese, grated
1 can tomato soup
1 large onion, chopped fine
1 egg, separated

1 tsp. salt
1 tsp. black pepper
1 tsp. dry mustard
1 tsp. Worcestershire

In top of double boiler (or chafing dish) saute chopped onions in butter until limp. Place top of boiler over boiling water and add tomato soup (do not add water to soup). After soup is hot gradually stir in grated cheese.

Stir all the above seasonings into the yolk of egg and add this mixture to the rarebit. Beat the white of egg and fold into the rarebit just before serving.

Serve on saltines or toast.

Any leftover may be refrigerated and used as cheese spread.

73

CAROLYN'S CHICKEN CASSEROLE

4 oz. chipped beef, rinsed and dried	4 oz. mushrooms sauteed
6 chicken breast, skinned and boned	10 1/2 mushroom soup
1 cup sour cream	dash of pepper

Preheat oven to 275 degrees. Sliced rolled chipped beef into 1/4 inch slices. and line the bottom of a 10 x 10 shallow greased casserole with the shredded beef. Place the breast on top of the beef. Sprinkle with pepper. Mix the soup and sour cream well and pour over the chicken breast. Cover with foil and bake for 3 hours. Serves 6.

MUSHROOM SAUCE

2 tbsps. butter or other fat	1 cup chicken broth
1/2 lb. mushrooms, sliced	1/4 tsp. salt
2 tbsps. flour	1/8 tsp. pepper

Melt butter, add mushrooms, and cook about 5 minutes. Blend in flour. Add chicken broth gradually; cook until thickened, stirring constantly; add seasonings and serve hot. Makes 1¾ cups.

PINEAPPLE MINT SAUCE

¾ cup crushed pineapple, canned	¾ cup water
1/4 cup pineapple juice	6 drops oil of peppermint
1 cup sugar	Green coloring

Place the pineapple, juice, sugar, and water into a saucepan, and cook about 10 minutes over a slow fire until thickened. Cool, and then add the oil of peppermint and coloring. Chill. Serve with roast lamb.

PLANTATION SHORTCAKE

4 inch square hot corn bread, split horizontally and buttered	1/4 cup diced cooked Virginia Ham
1/2 cup cream sauce made with equal amounts of chicken stock and rich milk	1/4 cup diced white meat of chicken

The corn bread may be baked in individual cakes, if desired. Mix sauce, ham, chicken and heat. Cover lower and top layers of corn bread with this spread. Serve immediately. Capers or sauteed mushrooms may be added.

MEATS

MAMA BET'S CHEESY CHICKEN BREAST

6 chicken breast	1 can cream of chicken soup
1 1/2 cup sour cream	1/2 lb. sharp cheese grated
1 tube ritz crackers, crushed	sesame seeds

Put chicken breast in water and boil until tender. Cool, debone and skin. Mix soup and sour cream well and pour over chicken. Sprinkle with grated cheese and top with cracker crumbs. Sprinkle with sesame seeds and bake uncovered for 45 minutes at 350 degrees. Serves six.

RAISIN SAUCE

¾ cup brown sugar	¼ cup vinegar
½ cup raisins	1 lemon, sliced thin
3 tbsps. cornstarch	1 tbsp. butter
1½ cups broth from ham or tongue	

Mix sugar and cornstarch together and gradually add the broth, stirring to prevent lumps. Pour into a double boiler and add the rest of the ingredients and cook until raisins are plump and mixture is thick. Serve hot on ham or tongue.

STUFFING FOR FOWL

1 loaf bread	1½ tsps. poultry seasoning
1 onion, chopped	1 egg beaten (optional)
1 cup diced celery	2 tbsps. margarine
Chopped cooked giblets	¾ cup giblet stock
1½ tsps. salt	

Cut bread into small pieces and let dry out over night. Also cook giblets. Add to bread chopped onion, celery, giblets, seasoning and egg. Bring giblet stock and margarine to a boil. Pour over other ingredients and cover tightly. Let stand about 10 minutes, then mix thoroughly.

SWEET SOUR SPARERIBS

Ingredients required for 4 servings.

1 tsp. salt
1/2 tsp. powdered ginger
1/3 cup brown sugar
1/2 cup vinegar
1/2 cup water

1 tbsp. soy sauce
2 lbs. lean pork spareribs, cut in approximately 2″ pieces
2 tbsps. cornstarch

Combine salt, ginger, sugar, vinegar, water and soy sauce. Pour over spareribs in a flat dish or bowl, in order to make sure that sauce reaches every piece of sparerib. Marinate over-night. Drain off marinade, bake spareribs on a broiler rack or in a baking pan with rack in a moderate oven, say for one hour at 350°F. Dissolve cornstarch in a very small amount of water and add to marinade in saucepan. Bring to boil, stir occasionally and boil about 5 minutes, or until the sauce is thickened. Pour over spareribs in serving dish.

TURKEY STUFFING

2 cups mashed potato
1½ cups ground bread crumbs
1/4 cup salt pork (ground)
1/3 cup butter (melted)
1 onion (cut fine)

1 egg
1 tsp. salt
Dash pepper
1/2 tsp. poultry seasoning

Five times this recipe fills a 20 pound bird. This is a very moist and delicious stuffing.

WILD RICE AND CHESTNUT STUFFING

1 cup wild rice
1/2 lb. chestnuts, blanched and cooked
1/2 cup melted butter, or other fat

1/4 tsp. salt
1/8 tsp. pepper
2 tbsps. minced onion

Wash rice thoroughly and steam, using 3 cups of water and 1 tsp. salt, for about 40 minutes, or until tender; drain. Add remaining ingredients and toss lightly. Fills a 4 lb. fowl.

To shell and blanch chestnuts; place the chestnuts in cold water, discard those which float. Dry and slit each shell ½ to ¾ inch on each side, place in saucepan, add 1½ tbs. cooking oil and shake pan over heat 5 minutes. Roast in 450°F oven for another 5 min. After cooling, remove shells and brown skin with sharp paring knife.

76

SEAFOOD

CRABMEAT IMPERIAL

1 lb. fresh lump crabmeat
1 cup heavy cream sauce
1 egg yolk (whole egg may be used)
¼ tsp. dry mustard
¼ tsp. paprika
1 heaping tsp. capers
1 tsp. worcestershire sauce

7 tbsp. mayonnaise (use 1 tbsp. in mixture balance to top crabmeat in shell)
½ tbsp. chopped pimento
½ tbsp. chopped green pepper
1 tbsp. butter
Salt & white pepper to taste

Saute the green pepper and pimento in butter. Add this to the cream sauce and all the other ingredients except the crabmeat. Mix well. Fold in the crabmeat last. Handle lightly. Place in oven (in natural crab shells) and put a tbsp. of mayonnaise on top of each portion. Bake in moderate oven for 20-30 minutes. Yields 6 servings.

BROILED SWORDFISH WITH ANCHOVIES

4 swordfish steaks
1/4 cup melted butter

Paprika
1 small can anchovies

Brush steaks well with butter. Sprinkle with paprika and place on pre-heated, greased broiler rack—450°F oven. Broil until golden brown and bubbly. Baste with pan drippings. Turn when half done. Sprinkle with paprika and place one anchovy on each steak. Pour anchovy oil over all. Broil about 4 min. Serves 4.

CRAB RAVIGOTE

1 lb. fresh backfin crabmeat
6 natural crab shells
1 tbsp. onion, chopped fine
1 tbsp. red pepper, chopped fine
1 tbsp. green olives, chopped fine
3/4 tbsp. dill pickle, chopped fine

1 tbsp. whipped cream
2 tbsps. mayonnaise
1 tsp. Worcestershire sauce
2 hard boiled eggs
3 sprigs parsley

Mix together all the ingredients (but the eggs and parsley) with mayonnaise which has been lightened with whipped cream. Fill crab shells and decorate with chopped parsley, chopped egg white, and chopped egg yolk. Serve on lettuce leaf with slice of tomato and lemon.

Yield: 6 servings.

INDIVIDUAL LOBSTER PIE

2 tbsps. butter
1 cup well-packed lobster meat
1/4 cup sherry
3 tbsps. butter

1 tbsp. flour
3/4 cup thin cream
2 egg yolks

Melt 2 tbsp. butter. Add sherry. Boil 1 min. Add lobster and let stand. Melt 3 tbsp. butter. Add flour. Stir until it bubbles 1 min. Remove from heat. Slowly stir in cream and wine drained from lobster. Return to heat and cook, stirring constantly until the sauce is smooth and thick. Remove from heat. Beat egg yolks very well. Stir into yolks 4 tbsp. of sauce, 1 tbsp. at a time. Add to sauce, mixing well. Heat over hot water in top of double boiler. Water should not be allowed to boil. If it does, sauce may curdle or break. Sauce should be stirred constantly while heating. It takes about 3 minutes. Remove from heat. Add lobster. Turn into small deep pie plate. Sprinkle with topping. Bake in slow oven 300°F for 10 minutes.

SEAFOOD

BAKED STUFFED SHRIMP

Use Jumbo Shrimp, allowing 3 shrimp per serving. Split shrimp through center. Stuff with the following mixture:

3 tbsps. finely chopped scallops
2 ozs. Chablis wine
2 cups cracker meal
1 tsp. paprika

2 tbsps. finely crushed potato chips
2 tsps. Parmesan cheese
2 tbsps. melted butter

Place in pan with little water—this prevents shrimp from drying. Bake 20 minutes at 325°F. This is sufficient to stuff 12 Jumbo Shrimp.

CRAB STEW

Meat from 1 dozen crabs
1 med. onion
1 lemon rind, thinly sliced
1 cup celery, thinly chopped
3 cups milk
1 tbsp. cornstarch

Juice 1 lemon just before serving
1/2 stick butter
Salt and pepper to taste
Sherry wine to taste, just before
    serving

Steam celery, onion and lemon rind until very tender and all water disappears. Add butter and saute' until slightly brown. Cook milk and cornstarch until it slightly thickens. Add crabmeat, saute' (salt and pepper to taste), cook about 10 minutes. Add lemon juice and wine just before serving.

ESCALLOPED CLAMS

Blend together well:
1 pt. warm milk
2 beaten eggs
2 cups cracker crumbs

1/2 cup margarine (reserve a little)
1 small onion cut fine

Salt and pepper to taste. Fold in 2 small cans minced clams and liquor. Pour into greased casserole. Dot with remaining butter. Bake 45 minutes at 350°F. Serves 6.

ESCALLOPED OYSTERS

1 qt. oysters	3 tbsps. finely chopped green pepper
1 cup cracker meal	Speck minced garlic
1/2 cup butter	2 tbsps. Worcestershire sauce
2 tbsps. flour	3 tbsps. lemon juice
3 tbsps. finely chopped onion	Salt and pepper to taste

Heat oysters in own juice. Brown flour and butter, pour over heated oysters. Add all seasoning and cracker meal. Bake at 375°F in casserole for 20-25 minutes. Leave in oven 1/2 to 3/4 hr. before serving.

FRIED SOFT SHELL CRABS

6 soft shell crabs	Flour
1 cup milk	Salt and pepper to taste

Remove the soft feeders or "dear men" under each side of the shell, remove eyes, mouth and sand bag under the mouth. Wash crabs well in cold water and dry on a towel. Season milk well with salt, pepper and soak the crabs in this mixture. Roll in a little sifted flour and fry until color of crabs turn red. Serve garnished with lemon slices and minced parsley.

OYSTER VIOLA

1 pt. oysters	Pinch of mace
1 can celery soup	1/4 lb. butter
1/2 cup minced onion	2 tbsps. curry
Black pepper	

Prepare soup and oysters separately. When soup has simmered, combine with hot oysters and juice and simmer until oysters begin to curl.

ROCKEFELLER OYSTERS

2 doz. oysters on half shell (1 pt.)	1/2 lb. butter
8 slices crisp fried bacon	Parsley, green onion tops, juice of 1
2 cups bread crumbs	lemon
1 lb. spinach	Salt and cayenne pepper to taste

If you use bulk oysters, put 1 or more on an oyster shell. Chop onion tops, parsley and cooked spinach and mix together with salt, butter, pepper and lemon juice. Put green mixture on each oyster, also crumble bacon and bread crumbs over the top. Put in hot oven and let stay until they swell.

SEAFOOD

SCALLOPED SCALLOPS

1 pt. scallops	1/2 cup soft bread crumbs
1/2 cup butter	2/3 cup cream or top milk
1 cup cracker crumbs	Salt and pepper

Wash and pick over scallops. Melt butter and add cracker crumbs and bread crumbs. Put layer of crumbs in buttered baking dish, cover with scallops, half the cream, and season; repeat; cover with buttered crumbs and bake about 25 minutes at 350°F.

SALMON CROQUETTES

2 cups water	1 tbsp. lemon juice
1 cup uncooked oatmeal	1 tsp. salt
1 1-lb. can salmon, drained, boned and flaked	1/4 tsp. pepper
	1 1/2 tsps. Worcestershire sauce

Stir rolled oats into boiling water. Cook slowly for 5 minutes, stirring often. Combine cooked oatmeal with remaining ingredients. Cool. Shape into 12 croquettes; roll in bread crumbs, then dip in beaten egg and roll again in crumbs. Fry in hot, deep fat 375°F til golden brown. Serve hot.

SCALLOPED OYSTERS

1 pt. oysters	2 eggs, slightly beaten
2 cups milk	2 cups cracker crumbs
1/2 cup melted butter	Salt and pepper

Cut the oysters (with scissors) once or more according to size. Beat eggs, add milk and seasonings. Grease a baking dish and add a layer of crumbs. Add a layer of oysters (1/2 pint). Add another layer of crumbs, then another of oysters. Pour over this the milk and egg and seasoning. Add a layer of crumbs and dot with melted butter. Bake for 20 minutes in hot oven—400°F. Makes 4 to 6 servings.

SHRIMP AND CRAB CASSEROLE

1 lb. crab meat
1 lb. shrimp, cooked and shelled
1 cup of diced celery
1/4 cup chopped green pepper

1 tsp. grated onion
1 cup mayonnaise
Salt and pepper to taste

Combine ingredients and put into a well greased casserole. Sprinkle with bread crumbs and paprika. Bake 30 minutes at 325°F.

SHRIMP CREOLE

2 cups of shrimp
1/2 lb. of ham
1 can tomato soup
2 large onions

1 small bell pepper
1 cup celery
1/4 stick of butter
Salt to taste

Saute ham, onions, celery, and bell pepper in the butter. Add soup and shrimp and cook slowly for one hour. Serve over cooked rice.

SHRIMP PIE

1 can tomatoes
1 cup bread crumbs
1 egg
1 tbsp. oil

Juice 1/2 lemon
1 1/2 cups prepared cooked shrimp, celery, soda, green pepper, onion and Worcestershire sauce

Put tomatoes to cook, after chopping fine, add pinch of soda, 2 table-spoons each of chopped celery, and green pepper, 1 tablespoon chopped onion, and bread crumbs. Cook 10 minutes, remove from stove. Add shrimp, beaten egg, oil, lemon juice, and dash of Worcestershire sauce. Place in buttered baking dish, sprinkle with bread crumbs, and bake 20 to 30 minutes in medium oven.

SHRIMP "RE DEGLI AMICI"

1 large can V-8 juice (16 oz.)
1 bay leaf
Juice of 1 lemon
1/2 tsp. each dried basil and oregano

3 dashes Tabasco
1 tbsp. vinegar
1 tbsp. Worcestershire sauce

Combine ingredients in frying pan and cook over medium high heat until reduced to the consistency of tomato paste. Add 2 or 3 pounds boiled shrimp, cleaned and veined. When shrimp are thoroughly hot, add 1/4 cup warmed brandy. Ignite and stir until flames die. Serves 4.

SEAFOOD

LOBSTER a la NEWBURG

4 tbsps. butter
1 cup mushrooms
2 cups milk
2 cups fresh heavy cream
Dash paprika

4 heaping tbsps. cracker crumbs
1/2 cup sherry wine
Salt and pepper
4 boiled lobster tails, diced

Saute mushrooms in butter until brown. Add milk, cream and salt and pepper. Let mixture come to a boil, then add cracker crumbs until it thickens. Stir in lobsters and sherry. Pour into casserole and sprinkle top with paprika. Put in 450°F oven about 1 minute and serve piping hot.

SEAFOOD DISH

1 lb. crab meat
1 lb. cooked shrimp
1 can artichoke hearts
1 pt. light cream
2 tbsps. butter
2 tbsps. flour
1 tsp. Worcestershire sauce

1 tsp. paprika
1 tbsp. lemon juice
2 tbsps. catsup
1 tbsp. Sherry wine
1 cup grated cheese
Salt and pepper to taste

Make cream sauce of cream, butter, flour and seasoning, adding cheese and wine last. Place in baking dish in layers—seafood, halves artichokes, cream sauce and repeat. Sprinkle bread crumbs over top and bake in 400°F oven about 20 minutes.

TROUT AMANDINE

6 filets trout
1 cup milk
1/2 cup flour, sifted

1/3 cup butter
1/2 cup almonds, chopped
Salt and pepper to taste

Dip filets in milk, roll in seasoned flour. Melt butter in skillet and brown filets evenly on both sides. Remove from skillet. Saute almonds. Pour browned butter and almonds over fish. Garnish with parsley and lemon wedges.

PERFECT DRESSING FOR FISH

1/4 cup butter	1 tsp. worcestershire sauce
1/2 cup onion, chopped	1/2 tsp. paprika
1/4 cup celery, chopped	1/2 tsp. old bay seasoning
1/4 cup green pepper, chopped	1/8 tsp. cayenne pepper
1/2 lb. small shrimp, cooked	1/4 cup dry sherry
1 tsp. parsley, chopped	1 1/2 cups bread crumbs
1 tsp. pimento, chopped	salt to taste

Melt butter and saute next three ingredients. Add remaining ingredients except bread crumbs and cook over low heat for about 10 minutes. Combine with bread and mix thoroughly. Stuff fish and brush with butter before baking.

ALMOND BUTTER SAUCE

1 lb. butter or Oleo	1 tbsp. parsley, chopped
5 ozs. pimento, chopped	1 tbsp. salt
5 ozs. almonds, chopped	1 tbsp. lemon juice

Saute almonds in butter slowly to a golden brown. Cool. Cream butter. Add finely chopped pimento, almonds, parsley, lemon juice and salt and mix thoroughly.

Yield: Using a tablespoon—24 servings.

"Remember! With seasonings, their restraint is their glory."

VEGETABLES

SOUTHERN SQUASH

6 or 8 tender, small squash
Salt and pepper to taste
2 tbsp. butter
1 bouillon cube
1 tbsp. grated onion

1 egg, well beaten
1 cup sour cream
1/2 cup breadcrumbs
1/2 cup grated cheese
Dash of paprika

Cut and cook squash until tender. Mash and add
salt, pepper, butter, bouillon cube and onion. Add
well beaten egg and sour cream. Pour into 1 quart
casserole dish. Combine breadcrumbs, grated
cheese, and paprika. Sprinkle over top of squash.
Bake at 350°F for 30 minutes.

SPINACH PARMESAN

4 lbs. fresh spinach	1/2 cup water
1/2 cup grated parmesan cheese	1/2 cup heavy cream
1/3 cup butter, melted	
1/3 cup onions, finely chopped	dash of pepper
1/3 cup dry breadcrumbs	

Wash spinach, pick and remove stems. Add water and cook over medium heat, covered for about 6-8 minutes. Drain and add all ingredients except breadcrumbs. Mix well and pour into a 10 x 11 inch shallow baking dish. Top with breadcrumbs and bake at 450 degrees for about 12-15 minutes. Serves six.

ASPARAGUS EN CASSEROLE

1 cup canned asparagus (cut in 2" pcs.)	1/4 cup melted butter
	1 beaten egg
1/2 tsp. salt	1/2 cup grated American cheese
1/8 tsp. pepper	3/4 cup finely rolled crackers
1/2 pimento, minced	1/2 cup milk

Combine all ingredients except butter. Pour into greased casserole and pour butter over top. Bake 20 to 30 minutes at 350°F.

BAKED CUCUMBERS

12 small cucumbers, peeled	1 cup milk
2 tbsps. butter	1/4 cup grated cheese
2 tbsps. flour	1/4 cup fine crumbs
3/4 tsp. salt	3/4 tsp. paprika
1/4 tsp. dry mustard	2 tbsps. vinegar

Cut the cucumbers in two lengthwise. Place them in a buttered casserole. Melt the butter and stir in the flour, mustard, salt and vinegar. Cook until well blended. Gradually add the milk and cook until thickened and smooth. Pour over the cucumbers. Mix the cheese, crumbs and paprika and ₃prinkle evenly over the top. Bake for 30 minutes at 350°F.

BROCCOLI WITH POPPY SEED SAUCE

1/2 cup butter, melted	2 tsps. lemon juice
2 tsps. poppy seeds	1 tbsp. cream

Melt the butter and remove from the fire before it bubbles. Mix with lemon juice, cream and poppy seeds. Good over asparagus, broccoli and carrots. Toasted sesame seeds may be used the same way.

VEGETABLES

CARROT-STICK CASSEROLE

6 medium carrots
3/4 cup water
3 tbsps. brown or maple sugar

3/4 tsp. salt
3 tbsps. butter

Cut carrots in thin strips. Put in casserole. Add water, salt, and sugar. Dot with butter. Cover. Bake 350°F about an hour. Serves 6.

CHEESE DRESSING

1/2 lb. cheese
1/2 cup cream

1 tsp. mustard
Salt to taste

Cook together, thickening with a little flour if necessary. Serve as sauce over asparagus, onions, cauliflower, or cabbage.

CORN OYSTERS

2 cups corn pulp
2 eggs separated
2 tbsps. flour

1/2 tsp. salt
1/4 tsp. pepper

To corn pulp, add beaten egg yolks, flour, and seasonings. Add stiffly beaten egg whites and blend. Drop by teaspoonfuls onto hot greased frying pan and brown on both sides. Serves 6.

COTTAGE-FRIED POTATOES

2 or 3 tbsps. cooking fat or oil
2 cups sliced cooked potatoes

Salt
Pepper

Heat fat or oil in a fry pan and add the potatoes. Season with salt and pepper.

Fry until potatoes are brown, turning them as they cook. 4 servings.

CRAB-STUFFED POTATOES

4 medium Idaho potatoes	1/4 tsp. cayenne
1 6 1/2 oz. can crabmeat	4 tbsps. grated onion
1/2 cup butter	1 cup grated sharp cheese
1/2 cup light cream	1/2 tsp. paprika
1 tsp. salt	

Scrub potatoes well and dry thoroughly. Bake in slow oven until you can pierce them easily with a fork.

Drain the crabmeat and pick it over. Cut the baked potatoes in half, lengthwise. Scoop out the potato and, with an electric mixer, whip the potato, butter, cream, salt, cayenne, onion and cheese. With a fork or spoon mix in the crabmeat and refill the potato shells. Sprinkle with paprika and reheat in a hot oven about 15 minutes.

These may be made in advance, frozen, and reheated in hot oven for about half an hour before serving.

CREAMED ARTICHOKES

6 French artichokes	Tabasco
1 cup cream	Salt and pepper
Lemon juice	

Boil six artichokes in water with salt and lemon juice. Scrape the leaves and put through a sieve. Heat in the top of double boiler. Add 1 cup of cream, salt to taste and a few drops of Tabasco. Add cleaned hearts just before serving.

CREAMED POTATOES

2 cups diced raw potatoes	1 tsp. salt
1 1/2 tbsps. butter	Pepper
1 1/2 tbsps. flour	1 cup milk

Cook potatoes in a small amount of boiling salted water until tender. Drain.

Melt the butter in a saucepan and blend in the flour, salt and pepper. Gradually stir in the milk and cook over low heat until thickened, stirring constantly.

Add the hot diced potatoes to the sauce. Reheat if necessary before serving. 4 servings.

VEGETABLES

PINEAPPLE CASSEROLE

3 cans pineapple (drained)
2 tbsp. flour
1 1/2 cup cheddar cheese

1 roll of ritz (crumbled)
2 tbsp. sugar

Mix half the cheese with all other ingredients. Place in buttered casserole dish and top with the other half of the cheese. Dot with butter and bake at 325 degrees for about 25 minutes. Serve hot.

HARVARD BEETS

2 cups boiled beets, cubed
1/3 cup sugar
1 tbsp. cornstarch
1/4 cup vinegar

1/4 cup water in which beets were cooked
1/2 tsp. salt
2 tbsps. butter, melted

Combine the cornstarch and sugar, add the beet water, vinegar and salt, and bring to a boil, stirring until thick and smooth. Add the beets and cook over a low fire for 20 minutes. When ready to serve, add the butter and bring to a boil.

HASH-BROWNED POTATOES

2 cups diced cooked potatoes
2 tbsps. finely chopped onion
4 tsps. flour
1 1/2 tsp. salt

Pepper
2 tbsps. milk
2 tbsps. cooking fat or oil

Combine potatoes and onion. Mix flour, salt and pepper, and slowly blend in the milk. Combine with the potato and onion mixture. Heat fat or oil in a heavy fry pan. Spread potato mixture evenly in the pan, making one large cake that does not touch the sides.

Cook over medium heat until the underside is brown. Cut into four equal portions and turn each piece to brown the other side. 4 servings.

CURRIED CABBAGE

5 cups shredded cabbage cooked in boiling salted water 10 to 15 minutes
4 tsps. butter, melted
4 tsps. flour
1/2 tsp. salt
3/4 tsp. curry powder
2 tbsps. minced onion
3/4 cup milk

Melt butter in top of double boiler. Add combined dry ingredients. Add milk gradually. Stir until thickened. Pour over cooked drained cabbage.

HOPPIN' JOHN

Traditional dish for New Year's Day.
1 cup blackeyed peas (1/2 lb.)
1 cup rice
1/2 lb. slab smoked bacon
Salt and pepper to taste

Cut bacon in small thin pieces and fry. Cook peas in 1 qt. cold water, adding grease from bacon to season. Add salt and cook until peas are soft but quite firm. You should have slightly more than 1 cup of juice. Add 1 cup of rice. It may be necessary to add small amount of boiling water while peas are cooking. Cook until mixture is dry, adding bacon in time to heat well, season with cayenne pepper.

HUNGARIAN CABBAGE

1 cup of celery juice or
1 10 1/2 oz. can condensed cream of celery soup, undiluted
1/2 cup sour cream
1/2 tsp. caraway seeds
1/2 tsp. salt
1 medium head of cabbage cut in wedges

In a 3 quart saucepan blend and heat soup, sour cream, caraway seeds and salt. Add cabbage; cover and cook over low heat 20 to 30 minutes or until cabbage is tender.

MASHED CREAMED BEETS

12 large beets
1/2 tsp. salt
1/2 medium sweet pepper, minced
1 tbsp. lemon juice
1/2 cup sour cream

Boil beets until tender. Press through ricer. Add seasoning and cream. Place in baking dish that has been rubbed with garlic. Cover with buttered crumbs and bake 20 minutes at 350°F.

VEGETABLES

INDIAN FRIED RICE

2 lbs. rice	¾ tsp. of ground cinnamon
4 medium sized onions	4 ozs. of butter or margarine
½ tsp. of powdered cloves	Salt to taste
½ tsp. of shelled cardamon seeds	3 pts. of water

Slice onions and fry in hot butter till a golden brown and remove. Fry spices in same butter till they crackle. Add rice and fry a few minutes. Add salt and water, cover and cook till all the water has been absorbed. Serve hot, garnished with sliced fried onions. Serves 8 portions.

EGGPLANT CASSEROLE

1 medium eggplant	1 cup cheddar cheese, grated
1/2 cup onion, chopped	1/2 cup croutons
1/4 cup green pepper, chopped	8 saltine crackers
3-4 tablespoons butter	2-3 tablespoons butter
1/2 teaspoon salt	1/8 tsp. pepper

Preheat oven to 350. Peel eggplant and cut in 1 inch cubes. Boil in 1 cup salted water until tender. Saute onions and green pepper in butter over low heat until tender. Stir in remaining salt, pepper, cheese and croutons. Remove from heat and add drained eggplant. Put mixture in buttered 1 1/2 quart casserole dish. Saute crumbled crackers in butter, coating well and place on top of casserole. Bake until bubbling hot for about 25 minutes. Serves 6.

PUFFED PAPRIKA POTATOES

5 potatoes	3 tsps. butter
½ tsp. paprika	2 or 3 tsps. tomato puree
1 tsp. salt	1 or 2 egg whites

Bake potatoes. Cut slice from top of each. Remove contents and press through potato ricer. Add remainder of ingredients except egg and beat until light. Fold in stiffly beaten egg whites. Refill cases lightly and brown in hot oven. Garnish with parsley.

CARROT-PECAN CASSEROLE

3 lb. carrots, sliced	2/3 cup sugar
1/2 cup butter, softened	1/2 cup chopped pecans, toasted
1/4 cup milk	2 eggs, beaten
3 tbsp. all-purpose flour	1 tsp. grated orange rind
1 tbsp. vanilla extract	1/4 tsp. nutmeg

Cook carrots in a small amount of water for 12 minutes and drain. Mash carrots and stir in all other ingredients. Pour into a lightly greased casserole and bake for 40 minutes at 350 degrees.

BROCCOLI WITH YOGURT

20 oz. frozen broccoli	1 lemon, juiced
1.2 cup fat free mayonnaise	butter flavored salt
1/2 cup fat free yogurt	bread crumbs

Preheat oven to 275. Cook broccoli and drain. Arrange in 1 1/2 quart baking dish. Mix mayonnaise, yogurt and lemon juice together and cover broccoli. Cover with butter flavored bread crumbs and bake for 20 minutes. Serves 6.

CHINESE BROCCOLI

1 tbsp. soy sauce	1/3 crushes red peppers
12 tbsp. rice vinegar	1/2 tsp. peeled, minced ginger
1/2 tsp. sugar	2 cloves garlic, minced
1 tbsp. sesame seeds	5 cups coarsely chopped broccoli

Combine soy sauce, rice vinegar and sugar in a small bowl and set aside. Heat a large skillet or wok over medium heat. Add sesame seeds and cook 1 minute or until browned. Remove seeds and set aside. Add oil and next three ingredients to skillet; stir-fry 30 seconds. Add broccoli; stir-fry 1 minute. Add soy sauce mixture and stir well. Cover and cook 3 minutes or until broccoli is tender. Sprinkle with sesame seeds. Serves 4.

VEGETABLES

SPINACH RING

2 boxes frozen chopped spinach	¼ small onion grated
3 tbsps. flour	1½ tbsp. lemon juice
3 tbsps. melted butter	Salt and pepper
3 beaten egg yolks	3 stiffly beaten egg whites

Cover and steam spinach in double boiler until thawed; add flour blended with butter. Add egg yolks, onion, lemon juice, and seasonings. Fold in egg whites. Pour into 10 inch greased ring mold. Bake in pan of hot water in moderate oven 350°F—30 to 45 minutes, or until set. Unmold on warm platter.

SWEET POTATO PUFFS

1 small sweet potato for each person	Few cut pecans and raisins
1 lump of butter	Marshmallows
brown sugar	Cornflakes
½ tsp. nutmeg—allspice, and cloves	

Cook and mash the sweet potatoes, add a large lump of butter while still hot, season with brown sugar, spices, raisins and pecans. When well mixed take marshmallows and mold the potato mixture around each marshmallow to form balls. Roll in cornflakes and fry in deep fat.

TURNIP CASSEROLE

To one medium-sized cooked and mashed turnip add:	3 tbsps. melted butter
1 large beaten egg	1 tsp. salt
¼ cup Cream of Wheat	Dash of pepper
	1 tbsp. sugar

Stir ingredients thoroughly and place in a well-greased 2 qt. casserole. Leave uncovered. Bake in 375°F oven for 30 minutes. Serve hot.

SWEET POTATOES

1/2 tsp. nutmeg	2 1/2 lb. dry pack sweet potatoes
1/4 tsp. cinnamon	1/4 lb. butter
3/4 cup sugar	2 cups milk
1 tsp. salt	

Mix together nutmeg, cinnamon, sugar and salt. Add sweet potatoes, butter and milk. Bake in a hot oven until glazed on top.

QUICK SCALLOPED POTATOES

2 cups thinly sliced raw potatoes	1 tsp. salt
1 1/2 cups milk	Pepper
1 tbsp. flour	1 tbsp. butter or margarine

Combine potatoes and milk and cook in a saucepan over low heat on top of the range for 15 to 20 minutes, taking care not to let the milk scorch.

Place a layer of potatoes in a greased baking dish, sprinkle with flour, salt and pepper. Repeat until all the potatoes are used.

Pour the milk left in the saucepan over the potatoes and dot with butter or margarine.

Cover and bake in a moderate oven (350°F) for 10 minutes, or until potatoes are tender. Remove cover and bake 10 minutes longer. If the potatoes are not brown enough on top, place the uncovered dish under the broiler for 3 or 4 minutes. 4 servings.

Dishes that simmer, or bubble or stew
For long patient hours—like soup or ragout—
Should be given their herbs the last hour or so,
For too lengthy cooking lets herb flavors go.

But dishes that cook while you hurry and fix,
Should receive their herb quota right in the mix;
While cold things—like cocktails—really should sleep
Overnight with their herbs to allow them to steep.

DESSERTS

PECAN CAKE

6 eggs, separated
1 lb. sugar
½ lb. butter
1 lb. shelled pecans
1 lb. seeded raisins
1 whole nutmeg, grated

½ pt. whiskey
1 lb. flour
1 tsp. baking powder
8 oz. candied cherries
1 lb. dates

Cover raisins with warm water and leave overnight. Next morning drain well. Sift flour and baking powder together; add fruits. Cream butter and sugar until light; add beaten yolks, and blend well. Add flour mixture and whiskey, alternately, to the butter, sugar, egg mixture beginning and ending with flour. Fold in stiffly beaten whites last. Bake 4 hours at 300°F.

RUBY'S BANANA NUT BREAD

2 cups mashed ripe bananas	1 cup chopped nuts
3 cups all-purpose flour	3 eggs beaten well
2 cups sugar	1 1/2 cups vegetable oil
1 tsp. soda	1 eight-ounce can crushed
2 tsp. vanilla extract	pineapple (drained well)
1 tsp. salt	1 tsp. cinnamon

Mix dry ingredients well. Stir in nuts and set aside.

Mix remaining ingredients and add to the dry ingredients.

Stir until completely moistened.

Pour into 3 loaf pans(9x5x3) and bake at 350 degrees for one hour and 5 minutes or until a toothpick inserted in the center comes out clean. Let pans sit for 10 minutes before removing loaves to wire racks. Cool before cutting.

BAKED APPLE DUMPLINGS

2 cups flour	1/2 cup shortening
4 tsp. baking powder	6 apples, peeled and cored
1/2 tsp. salt	1 cup sugar
2 tbsps. sugar	1 cup water
3/4 cup milk	1 tbsp. of butter

Mix flour, baking powder, salt and two tablespoons sugar. Work in shortening with tips of fingers, and add milk quickly. Toss on floured board, roll and cut in six inch squares. Place an apple on each, with one tablespoon sugar. Bring up corners, twist and pinch together and place side by side in a well greased pan. Pour over water and remaining sugar and bake in a hot oven about 45 minutes until crisp and well done. Serve hot with sauce in pan or brandy sauce.

Brandy Sauce: Cream 1/2 cup of butter with 1 cup of sugar. Stir over hot water till the butter and sugar blend and melt. Add 1 egg beaten well with a little water. Stir until thick. Then add brandy to flavor.

DESSERTS

BAKED ALASKA

1 9-inch square layer cake (sponge or butter or frozen cake)
1 layer of ice cream (have very hard) to cover center of cake to 1″ of edge

4 egg whites
½ cup sugar
Salt

Preheat oven to 400°F (moderately hot). Beat egg whites until firm. Add sugar and salt and beat until very stiff. Place cake on a thick board and quickly put ice cream on top and cover with meringue. Be sure to seal meringue to sides of cake. Bake until meringue is brown. Serve at once.

BAKED DEVIL FLOAT

1 cup sugar
2 cups water
2 tbsps. Crisco
½ cup sugar
3 tbsps. cocoa
½ cup milk

1 cup flour
Salt
½ cup nuts (optional)
2 tsps. baking powder
2 tsps. vanilla

Boil 1 cup sugar and water. Cream shortening and ½ cup sugar. Add dry ingredients: alternate with milk. Add nuts. Drop from spoon into boiling syrup. Bake 30 minutes at 350°F. Serve with whipped cream or ice cream.

BLACKBERRY PUDDING

Mix 1 tbsp. butter
1 cup sugar
1 egg

½ cup sifted flour
1 tbsp. baking powder

Boil 2 quarts blackberries and add to above. Bake in 350°F oven for 45 minutes. Serve with brown sugar, hard sauce, sprinkled with nutmeg.

BAKED FRUIT COMPOTE

5 medium bananas
1/2 cup unpeeled diced red apples
1/3 cup fresh orange juice
3 tbsps. fresh lemon juice

1/4 cup strained honey
1/2 cup grated fresh coconut
Orange slices for garnish

Cut bananas into ½" thick slices. Place in a 1-quart casserole along with the apples. Combine orange and lemon juice and honey. Pour over fruit. Place in a preheated hot oven (400°F) for 10 minutes or until fruit is tender. Sprinkle coconut over the top and bake 5 minutes longer or until coconut is lightly browned. Garnish with orange slices. Serve warm. Makes 6 servings.

BAKED INDIAN PUDDING

1 qt. milk
1/2 cup yellow corn meal
1/4 cup sugar
1 tsp. salt
1 tsp. cinnamon

1/2 tsp. ginger
1 egg
1/2 cup molasses
2 tbsps. butter

Scald 3 cups of milk in top of double boiler, remove from heat. Stirring constantly, slowly blend in corn meal, sugar, salt, cinnamon and ginger. Vigorously stir about 3 tsp. of the hot mixture into a mixture of egg, well beaten and molasses. Blend this into the hot corn meal mixture and cook over boiling water about 10 minutes, or until very thick; stir constantly. Beat in butter and turn mixture into thoroughly buttered casserole. Pour over top 1 cup cold milk. Bake at 300°F about 2 hours, or until the top is brown. Serve pudding warm with cream.

BAKED LEMON PUDDING

3 tbsps. butter or margarine
5 tbsps. flour
1 cup sugar

2 eggs, separated
1 cup milk
1 lemon, grated rind and juice

Cream butter or margarine. Add flour and ¾ cup sugar. Mix well.
Beat egg whites, add ¼ cup sugar and fold into first mixture. Pour into greased 2 qt. casserole. Place in a pan of hot water. Bake at 350°F for 40 min. Cool, unmold upside down and serve with whipped cream or lemon sauce.

DESSERTS

BLACKBERRY ROLL

2 cups blackberries	1 egg
¾ cup sugar	1 rounded tbsp. lard
2 cups of flour, sifted	1 cup or less of water, sufficient for a
½ tsp. salt	soft dough
2 tsps. baking powder	

Mix the pastry and roll it thin, about ¼ inch thick. Meanwhile, sprinkle 2 cups of blackberries with ¾ cup of sugar. Spread the berries on the dough and roll it up pinching the ends to seal completely. Place the roll in the center of a square of wet cloth and tie the corners to form a bag. Lower the bag into a pan of boiling water and boil for 45 minutes. Never let the boiling stop. Remove roll from the bag and place on a platter. Slice to serve and pour brandy sauce generously over each slice. This may be baked in the oven at 325°F with water in the pan so that the roll does not dry out.

BLUEBERRY CRISP PUDDING

4 cups fresh blueberries*	1/3 cup brown sugar, firmly packed
1/3 cup granulated sugar	1/3 cup sifted all purpose flour
2 tsps. lemon juice	¾ cup quick-cooking oats
4 tbsps. butter or margarine	

*Substitute 2 15-oz. cans drained, syrup packed blueberries and 1/3 cup syrup. Omit granulated sugar.

Place berries in a 1½ quart baking dish. Sprinkle with granulated sugar and lemon juice. Cream butter or margarine; gradually add brown sugar. Blend in flour and oats with fork. Spread topping over blueberries. Bake in a moderate oven (375°F) 35 to 40 minutes. Serve with plain or whipped cream. Yield: 6 servings.

MERINGUE

3 egg whites	2 tbsps. cocoa or 1½ sq. chocolate
1/3 cup sugar	melted

Spread meringue on pudding and return to oven. Serve hot.

99

BISHOP TUCKER'S BATTER PUDDING

1 cup milk
1 heaping tsp. butter
1/2 cup flour

3 eggs
Pinch of salt

Put the milk in double boiler. When hot add the butter, bring to boil then add flour. Beat hard until the batter becomes smooth & leaves the sides of the pan. Remove from fire & gradually beat in the beaten eggs (yolks & whites together) with salt. Turn into warm greased pan. May stand some time in warm kitchen before baking, but should be served as soon as done as it will fall. Bake in moderate oven. Pan may be set in hot water to keep from baking too fast. It should puff up like large popover with brown crust. Serve with wine or hard sauce. This makes a small pudding.

BREAD PUDDING

Bread
3 yolks of egg
1 qt. milk
1/2 cup raisins
Pinch of salt

1 cup sugar
1 tsp. lemon
1/2 tsp. nutmeg
1 tsp. butter

Break bread into small pieces to fill medium-sized casserole 2/3 full. Beat yolks, add sugar, melted butter, lemon, salt, and nutmeg. Pour into baking dish and bake with cover about 2 to 2½ hrs. Remove and add chocolate meringue.

CARAMEL BREAD PUDDING

1/2 cup sugar melted
4 cups scalded milk
2 cups stale bread crumbs
2 eggs

2/3 cup sugar
1/2 tsp. salt
1 tsp. vanilla

Melt ½ cup sugar in pan over hot fire, stirring constantly until color of maple syrup. Add syrup slowly to scalded milk in double boiler. When caramel has dissolved remove from fire, add stale bread crumbs and let soak for 30 min. Beat 2 eggs slightly, add sugar, salt, and vanilla & add to first mixture. Turn into a buttered baking dish and bake 1 hour in moderate oven. Cover with meringue and serve with cream.

DESSERTS

BROILED WALNUT FROSTING

2½ tbsps. butter
½ cup firmly packed brown sugar

2 tbsps. cream
½ cup chopped nuts

Melt butter, add remaining ingredients and blend well. Spread on warm cake. Put under broiler and broil until bubbly. Broil 3 or 4 inches away from heat. Watch it!!

CHERRY CREAM SHERBET

6 tbsps. lemon juice
1 tbsp. lemon rind
2/3 cup milk

1 cup cream
1/3 cup cherries cut fine
2 tsps. cherry juice

Combine juice, rind and sugar. Beat until well blended; then slowly add to milk continuing to beat. Add remaining ingredients. Pour into tray and stir about every ½ hour.

CHOCOLATE FUDGE

1 cup brown sugar
1 cup white sugar
⅛ lb. chocolate
1 tsp. butter
¾ cup milk

¼ cup cream
1 white of egg
1 tsp. vanilla
Nuts

Mix sugar, chocolate, milk, and cream. Cook until it forms a soft ball in water. Take off fire. Add butter, vanilla and nuts. When nearly stiff, beat into beaten white of egg. Pour into flat platter or pan. When hard cut into small blocks.

CHOCOLATE WAFFLES

3½ cups cake flour	2 cups milk
6 tsps. baking powder	4 ozs. chocolate
4 tsps. sugar	½ cup melted shortening
4 eggs	Dash of cinnamon or vanilla

Sift flour and sugar together twice. Add milk and beaten egg yolks. Add melted chocolate and beat until lumps disappear. Add baking powder sifted with a very small quantity of flour. Add beaten egg whites. When well folded in, bake in hot waffle iron 2½ min. Serve with flavored whipped cream or ice cream.

CHOCOLATE CHIFFON DESSERT

1 envelope unflavored gelatin	3 eggs, separated
½ cup sugar, divided	1½ cups milk
⅛ tsp. salt	1 tsp. vanilla
1/3 cup cocoa	Whipping cream, optional

Mix gelatin, ¼ cup of the sugar, salt, and cocoa in top of double boiler. Beat egg yolks and milk together. Add to gelatin. Cook over boiling water, stirring constantly until gelatin is dissolved, about 5 minutes. Remove from heat and stir in vanilla. Chill to unbeaten egg white consistency. Beat egg whites until stiff. Beat in remaining ¼ cup sugar. Fold chocolate gelatin mixture into egg whites. Turn into a 4 cup mold or individual molds. Chill until firm. Unmold on serving plate and garnish with whipped cream, if desired. Makes 8 servings.

CHOCOLATE MOUSSE

1 large can evaporated milk	1 tsp. vanilla
½ cup chocolate sauce	¼ tsp. salt

Chill canned milk before beating. Whip milk until stiff. Fold in chocolate sauce, vanilla, and salt. Freeze in deep tray without stirring.

CHOCOLATE SAUCE

2 cups sugar	1 cup water
1 tbsp. corn syrup	1 tbsp. butter
¼ tsp. salt	½ cup cocoa

Mix all ingredients together in saucepan. Stir over low heat until dissolved. Boil 5 minutes, add 1 tsp. vanilla and cool.

DESSERTS

CHOCOLATE SOUFFLE

1½ ozs. unsweetened chocolate	¾ cup milk
1/3 cup sugar	¼ tsp. salt
2 tbsps. hot water	3 egg yolks beaten until thick
2 tbsps. butter	3 egg whites
2 tbsps. flour	½ tsp. vanilla

Melt chocolate in double boiler. Add water and ½ of sugar portion. Melt butter in separate pan. Add flour. Blend the two and then add milk. Stir and cook until boiling point. Add chocolate mixture and then salt. Then add egg yolks and let mixture cool. Then, in separate bowl beat the 3 egg whites, adding remainder of sugar portion. Fold stiff egg whites into chocolate mixture. Add salt and vanilla. Then turn entire mixture into 2 qt. pyrex dish, and place pyrex dish in frying pan (or another large oven dish) containing 1 cup (more or less) of water. Put this in oven preheated to 325°F and bake for 30 to 40 minutes in a quiet kitchen. Serve this hot, with a very liberal amount of whipped cream as a side dish to be used as a sauce.

COFFEE FLUFF

1 envelope unflavored gelatin	1 tsp. vanilla
2 tbsps. sugar	2 egg whites
2 tsps. instant coffee	¼ cup sugar
¼ tsp. salt	¼ cup cold water
2 egg yolks	¼ cup nonfat dry milk
1¾ cups water	1 tsp. lemon juice

Mix gelatin, sugar, coffee, and salt together in the top of a double boiler. Beat together egg yolks and water. Add to gelatin mixture and cook over boiling water, stirring constantly until gelatin is dissolved, about 8 minutes. Remove from heat; add vanilla. Chill to unbeaten egg white consistency. Beat egg whites until stiff; beat in ¼ cup sugar. Fold in gelatin mixture. Beat cold water, dry milk, and lemon juice together until stiff and mixture stands in peaks. Fold into gelatin mixture. Turn into a 5-cup mold or individual dessert dishes. Chill until firm. Makes 8 servings.

FRUIT JUICE SNOW

1 envelope unflavored gelatin	1 can (6 oz.) frozen fruit juice
1/2 cup sugar	concentrate of your choice)
1/8 tsp. salt	2 unbeaten egg whites
1 1/4 cups water, divided	

Mix gelatin, sugar, and salt thoroughly in a small saucepan. Add ½ cup of the water. Place over low heat, stirring constantly until gelatin is dissolved. Remove from heat and stir in remaining ¾ cup of water and frozen fruit juice. Add unbeaten egg whites and beat with an electric beater until mixture begins to hold its shape or beat with a rotary beater until mixture is light and fluffy, about 7 minutes. To speed up hand beating place over ice and water; beat. Spoon into dessert dishes and chill until firm. Serve plain or with Custard Sauce. Makes 8 servings.

*If fresh or frozen pineapple juice is used, boil 2 min. before combining with the gelatin.

Custard Sauce

1 1/2 cups milk	3 tbsps. sugar
2 egg yolks	1/8 tsp. salt
1 whole egg	1 tsp. vanilla

Scald milk in top of double boiler. Beat egg yolks and egg, stir in sugar and salt. Gradually add small amount of hot milk, stirring constantly. Return to double boiler and cook, stirring constantly over hot, not boiling, water until mixture coats spoon. Remove from heat; cool. Stir in vanilla.

FRUIT SHERBET

1 pkg. fruit gelatin	1 tbsp. grated lemon rind
1 1/2 cups sugar	1 qt. milk (whole, skim, or 3 cups
2 cups boiling water	water and 1 cup dry milk plus 2
1/3 cup lemon juice or 1 cup crushed	tbsps. lemon juice)
fruit	

Mix gelatin and sugar. Add boiling water and stir until dissolved. Cool. Add lemon juice and rind. Stir cooled gelatin mixture into the milk. Freeze until mushy. Beat in a chilled bowl until smooth but not melted. Return to tray to harden. Makes 12 servings. (When using dry milk, put water and lemon juice into a large bowl, add milk powder, and beat with a rotary beater until well-mixed).

DESSERTS

RUM BALLS

2 cups vanilla wafers (crushed fine)
2 tablespoons cocoa
1 1/2 cups confectioner's sugar
2 tbsp. white corn syrup

1 cup pecans, chopped
very fine
1/4 cup rum

Mix vanilla wafer crumbs, cocoa, 1 cup confectioner's sugar and pecans well. Add corn syrup and rum mixing well. Shape into 1-inch balls and roll in remaining confectioner's sugar. Put in tightly covered container for at least 12 hours before serving.

To make Bourbon Balls, just follow the recipe above and substitute 1/4 cup bourbon for the rum. These keep for a good month.

ORANGE SHERBET

3 cups sugar
2 cups light corn syrup
2 cans of 12 oz. frozen orange
juice concentrate

2 six oz. cans frozen lemonade concentrate
rind of 2 oranges, grated

Boil sugar in 12 cups of water for 5 minutes and add corn syrup, juices and rind. Cool and strain. Pour mixture into 2 gallon freezer and follow the manufacturer's directions for freezing.

FROZEN PUDDING

3 eggs
1/2 pint whipping cream
3 tbsps. whiskey

Small box vanilla wafers
1/2 cup sugar

Whip cream—separate eggs—whip yolks until light and whites until stiff. Add sugar to yolks and cook in double boiler until thick. Then add whiskey and fold in cream and egg whites (beaten stiff). Crush wafers and put half in freezing tray—add pudding and cover with other half. Freeze.

FROZEN EGGNOG

4 eggs	1/4 cup bourbon
1/2 cup sugar	1/4 cup brandy
1 pint heavy cream	

To mix—add sugar to yolks, stir well, then bourbon and brandy—then cream whipped and last whites of eggs whipped stiff. Freeze and do not stir.

GREAT-GRAN'S ORANGE WATER ICE

1 pt. orange juice	1 cup sugar
Juice of 2 or 3 lemons	1 cup water

Boil sugar and water to form syrup. Cool, add juices. Pour into freezing tray. Using a silver fork, stir frequently while freezing.

HEAVENLY HASH

1 large can of pineapple	1/4 lb. of shelled pecans
1/3 lb. of malaga grapes	1/2 pt. cream
1/2 lb. of marshmallows	

Cut pineapple in small pieces. Cut grapes in halves and seed. Cut marshmallows in fourths and soak in milk 1/2 hour and drain. Chop nuts slightly. Whip cream. Drain fruit. Mix all ingredients well, and keep cold. This will serve 12 or 14 persons.

ICE BOX PUDDING

3 squares chocolate	Whites of 4 eggs
1 cup sugar	1 tsp. vanilla
1/2 cup boiling water	2 doz. lady fingers
Yolks of 4 eggs, beaten light	

Melt chocolate and remove from fire; add sugar and boiling water; fold in beaten yolks, then whites beaten stiff; add vanilla. Pour over one layer or one dozen lady fingers, place other layer and pour remainder of sauce. Let stand in ice box 24 hours. Serve with lots of whipped cream.

DESSERTS

LEMON BUTTER

2 eggs
2 tsp. butter

1 cup sugar
2 lemons (rind and juice)

Beat eggs; add sugar; beat again. Add butter, then lemon juice and grated rind. Cook until thick stirring constantly.

To be used as cake filling, or by adding another egg and leaving out the butter it can be used for dessert, serving with whipped cream.

LEMON ICE CREAM

Juice of 5 lemons
2 cups sugar

1 lemon sliced thin
1 qt. 20% cream

Add sugar to lemon juice, let stand until dissolved. Add sliced lemon to juice, add cream and freeze. Serves 8.

LEMON MILK SHERBET

3 or 4 lemons according to size
3 or 4 cups sugar

3 pts. milk
1 or 2 eggs

Cook lemons and sugar; beat eggs, add and stir into milk.

LEMON PUDDING

1 tsp. gelatin
4 eggs

1 cup sugar
2 lemons

Dissolve gelatin in 1 cup boiling water. Separate eggs, beat yolks till thick and creamy. Slowly adding sugar. Last, add cooled gelatin. Beat egg whites till stiff, add juice of 2 lemons, grated rind of one. Mix and cut into other mixture. Set to cool in serving bowl. Bottom is clear, top frothy.

LEMON SPONGE PUDDING

2 lemons, juice and rind	¾ cup sugar
3 eggs	1 tbsp. soft butter
2 tbsps. flour	1 cup milk

Add the grated rind and the lemon juice to the egg yolks and beat until thick. Mix the flour with the sugar. Stir into the egg and lemon mixture. Blend in the butter. Add the milk gradually. Beat the egg whites till stiff and fold into the mixture. Pour into a casserole or individual baking cups. Set in a pan of hot water and bake at 350°F for 30 minutes. May be served hot or cold.

MACAROON PARFAIT

¾ cup macaroon crumbs	½ pt. cream whipped
¾ cup top milk	½ tsp. vanilla
¼ cup sugar	¼ tsp. almond extract
Few grains salt	

Combine ½ cup macaroon crumbs with milk, sugar, and salt. Soak 1 hour. Fold in whipped cream and flavoring. Put in freezing pan of frigidaire. Cover with remaining crumbs. Freeze 4 hours.

Serve with or without whipped cream. This will freeze without forming crystals so often found in frozen desserts.

MAPLE SUGAR ICE CREAM

1 scant cup of maple sugar
8 eggs
1 quart cream

Dissolve sugar in double boiler. Add yolks of eggs and let cook until coats spoon. Take off fire and let cool, then add beaten egg whites and whipped cream and freeze.

PINEAPPLE OR PEACH SHERBET

2 cups buttermilk	1 cup crushed pineapple or mashed
1 cup sugar	peaches
	1 tbsp. vanilla

Mix together all ingredients. Freeze to a mush. Beat well and refreeze.

DESSERTS

OLD ENGLISH PLUM PUDDING

1/2 lb. beef suet (grated)	Pinch of salt
2 ozs. flour	1/4 lb. mixed peel
1/2 lb. raisins	1/2 lb. bread crumbs (fine)
1/2 lb. sultanas	2 ozs. coconut (shredded)
1/4 lb. currants	1 gill milk
1/2 nutmeg (grated)	1 wine glass rum or brandy
1/2 oz. ground cinnamon	1 lemon (strain juice, grate rind)
Pinch of allspice	4 eggs

Mix well together. Put in greased bowl and steam six hours tightly covered. Serve with hard sauce.

PECAN CONFECTIONS

1 egg white	1 level tbsp. flour
1 cup brown sugar	1 cup chopped pecans
1 pinch salt	

Beat egg white to a stiff froth, add gradually brown sugar, salt, flour. Stir in chopped pecans, drop on greased tins by small spoonfuls far apart. Bake in a very slow oven 15 minutes. Remove from tin when partly cooled. Makes 2 Dozen.

SNOWY COCONUT PUDDING

1 cup sugar	1 tsp. vanilla
1 envelope (1 tbsp.) unflavored gelatin	1 3 1/2-oz. can (1 1/4 cups) flaked coconut
1/2 tsp. salt	2 cups cream or canned milk
1 1/4 cups milk	Crimson Raspberry Sauce

Mix sugar, gelatine, salt and milk thoroughly. Stir over medium heat until sugar and gelatine dissolve. Chill until partially set. Add vanilla, and fold in coconut and then whipped cream. Pour into 1 1/2 quart mold and chill until firm, at least 4 hours. Unmold. Serve with Crimson Raspberry Sauce. Makes 8 servings.

PLAIN PUDDING SAUCE

1 heaping tsp. butter
2 tsp. flour
1½ cups hot water

1½ cups brown sugar
2 tsps. lemon juice
Pinch of nutmeg

Melt butter and add flour and hot water. Cook as for drawn butter and then add brown sugar. Stir until sugar is melted. Add lemon juice and nutmeg.

QUICKY LEMON FREEZE

1 cup evaporated milk (chilled)
1 tsp. salt
1 small can frozen lemonade

Whip cold milk, add lemonade and salt, and freeze. This can be made with frozen orange or grape juice, too.

SHERRY PUDDING

6 egg yolks
2 cups sugar
2 cups sherry

1 pt. whipping cream
1 tsp. vanilla
2 pkgs. knox gelatin

Soak gelatine until dissolved. Whip yolks, sugar and cream together. Add sherry, vanilla and gelatine. Put in mold, then in ice box. Garnish with jelly.

TYLER PUDDING

Sherwood Forest is the ancestral home of the Tyler family and this recipe was such a favorite with President Tyler that it carries his name. This pudding is a pie for it is baked on a pastry and one fourth of the recipe is sufficient for a smaller family.

1 fresh coconut (grated)
6 eggs (large)
5 cups sugar

1 cup thick cream
½ cup butter
Pie pastry, uncooked

Cream butter and sugar. Add eggs, well-beaten; then add the cream and last the coconut. Pour into four pie pans (9 inch). Place in preheated 300°F oven and bake for 15 or 20 minutes (or until done).

CAKES, PIES & COOKIES

RUM CREAM PIE

5 egg yolks
1 cup sugar
1 envelope unflavored gelatin
1/2 cup cold water

1 1/2 cups heavy cream
5 tbsp. dark rum
unsweetened chocolate crumb crust (dark Chocolate is best)

Beat egg yolks until white and add sugar. Soak gelatin in cold water; put gelatin and water over low heat, until dissolved. Pour over sugar and egg mixture, stirring briskly. Whip cream until stiff, fold into the egg mixture, and flavor with rum to taste. Cool until the mixture begins to set, and pour into pie shell. Chill until firm. Sprinkle top generously with shaved bitter-sweet chocolate curls. Garnish with whipped cream, if desired, and serve cold.

Yield 1 Pie.

ANGEL SPONGE

1 layer angel food cake
1 pkg. lemon instant pudding or other
flavor (butterscotch, coffee,
chocolate)
1 pt. heavy cream

Cut cake in 3 layers, put together with generous layers of pudding filling, ice with whipped cream and put in refrigerator for several hours.

APPLE SAUCE CAKE

1/2 cup butter or margarine
1 cup sugar
1 beaten egg
1/2 cup dates, cut fine
1 cup chopped seeded raisins
1 1/2 cups bread flour

1 tsp. soda
1 cup apple sauce
1/4 tsp. salt
2 tsp. cinnamon
1/2 tsp. nutmeg and allspice

Cream the butter and sugar. Add egg, dates and raisins. Mix the dry ingredients together and add to creamed mixture. Then work in apple sauce. Bake in slow oven 325°F about one hour.

BANANA CUP CAKES

2 cups sifted flour
2 tsps. baking powder
1/4 tsp. soda
1/2 tsp. salt
1/2 cup shortening
1 cup sugar
2 eggs, beaten

1 tsp. vanilla
1 tsp. lemon rind
1 tsp. orange rind
1 cup mashed, ripe bananas
2 tbsps. milk
1/2 cup chopped nuts

Grease 18 muffin pan sections or line with fluted baking cups. Sift together flour, baking powder, soda, salt. Cream together sugar and shortening until fluffy. Blend in beaten eggs, stir in vanilla, and orange and lemon rinds. Add flour mixture alternately with bananas and milk. Fold in nuts. Fill tins about 2/3 full and bake in 350°F oven for about 25 minutes.

CAKES, PIES & COOKIES

BABA AU RHUM

2 eggs
4 tbsps. sugar
¾ cup flour

2 tsps. baking powder
4 tbsps. milk

Mix eggs and sugar in mixer until the mixture becomes smooth and creamy. Add flour, milk, baking powder. Pour batter in crown shaped pan well buttered. Bake at 350°F for 15 to 20 minutes or until the cake looks golden in color. (Test with toothpick).

SAUCE: The cake once baked must be turned on serving dish, then the hot sauce poured on the hot cake. Put ingredients of sauce in pan on stove at the time you begin to make the cake. Bring sauce to boil then let simmer while the cake is baking.

2 cups water
1½ cups sugar
2 slices lemon (to be removed after cooking)

At the last minute add to this syrup:
¾ cup rum (Porto Rican dark)

As a finishing touch, spread apricot jam on top crown of baba.

BUTTERNUT CAKE

1 cup butter
2 cups sugar
3 cups flour
4 eggs

1 cup milk
1½ tsp. vanilla or lemon flavoring
½ tsp. salt
2 tsps. baking powder
1 cup butternuts

Soften the butter, cream till smooth, adding gradually half the sugar. Add the remaining sugar to well beaten egg yolks. Combine with butter mixture. Sift dry ingredients, add to first mixture alternately with milk. Add flavoring and egg whites beaten very stiff. Add one cup broken butternuts. Baked walnuts are also delicious. Bake in round loaf for 35-40 minutes at 350°F. When cool, frost.

HEAVENLY ANGEL CAKE

1 (10 oz.) angel food cake
3 cups whipping cream, divided
1/4 cup sifted powdered sugar

1/2 cup semisweet chocolate morsels
1 tablespoon raspberry liqueur

Slice off top 1/3 of cake and set aside. Using a sharp knife, hollow out the center of remaining cake, leaving a 1-inch shell. Place cake shell on serving plate and set aside.

Melt chocolate morsels in a heavy saucepan over low heat, stirring occasionally, until smooth. Remove from heat and let cool. Beat 1 cup whipping cream until firm peaks form; fold in liqueur and melted chocolate. Spoon into cake shell and place top 1/3 of cake over filling, pressing firmly.

Beat remaining 2 cups whipping cream until foamy; add powdered sugar, beating until firm peaks form. Spread over top and sides of cake. Chill up to 8 hours. Garnish with fresh raspberries.

EASY CHOCOLATE CAKE

2 cups cake flour
1 tsp. soda
¾ tsp. salt
1½ cups sugar
½ cup Crisco

1 tsp. vanilla
1¼ cups milk
2 eggs
3 squares chocolate

Sift flour, add soda, salt, sugar, and sift again into a large bowl. Drop in Crisco, add vanilla to the milk and pour ¾ cup of the milk into the bowl. Beat 2 minutes. Add the remaining milk and unbeaten eggs, and melted chocolate. Beat 1 minute longer. Turn into cake pans and bake in moderate oven 350°F.

LEMON SPONGE

1 cup evaporated milk, thoroughly
  chilled
1 envelope gelatine
2/3 cup hot water

2/3 cup sugar
Juice of 2 lemons
Grated rind of 1 lemon
2 cups vanilla wafers, crumbled fine

Thoroughly chill milk. Soak gelatine in cold water. Dissolve in hot water. Add sugar and lemon juice and rind. Cover bottom of biscuit pan with half of vanilla wafer crumbs, saving other half for topping. When jell is cool whip milk as stiff as it will become, add gelatine mixture a little at a time whipping as it is added. Pour on wafer crumbs, cover with remaining crumbs, and set in refrigerator until firm. Cut in squares to serve. This will keep several days, but will melt if left out of ice box too long. (Serves 6)

CAKES, PIES & COOKIES

BLACK WALNUT CAKE

2 cups sugar
1 cup butter or half margarine
3 cups flour
1 cup cold water

4 eggs
2 small tsps. baking powder
2 cups black walnuts

Beat white and yolks together, cream butter and sugar. Add to this the eggs. Beat hard before putting in the flour and baking powder. Add water last. Bake in tube pan in a slow oven 375°F for 1 hour or until done.

DEVIL'S FOOD CAKE

1½ cups sugar
½ cup butter
3 eggs

½ cup cocoa dissolved in
1 cup strong boiling coffee
2 cups flour
1 tsp. soda dissolved in a little water

Cream butter, add sugar, then egg yolks. Next add the cocoa and coffee mixture, cooled. Then soda and flour. Fold in beaten egg whites last. Bake in layers and put together with 7 min. frosting.

GOLDEN FRUIT CAKE

½ cup butter
1 cup sugar
¾ cup candied orange peel
¾ cup candied lemon peel
¾ cup candied citron peel
1 cup coconut, chopped
1 cup nuts, chopped

1 cup white raisins
2 cups flour
1 tsp. baking powder
½ tsp. salt
½ tsp. soda
3 eggs
½ cup orange juice

Cream butter. Add sugar. Add lightly beaten eggs and beat thoroughly. Add orange juice, peel, raisins, coconut and nuts. Fold in sifted dry ingredients. Pour into paper-lined, greased angel cake pan. Bake 2 to 2½ hours at 300°F.

115

DATE CAKE

1 cup chopped dates	1 tsp. vanilla
1 tsp. soda	1 cup boiling water
1 tsp. butter	1 cup sugar
Pinch of salt	1½ cups flour
1 egg	½ cup nut meats

Sprinkle soda over the chopped dates. Add boiling water. Let stand until cool, then add other ingredients. Bake in moderate oven 25 or 30 min.

FILLING FOR LEMON TARTS

4 eggs	1 tsp. flour
2 cups sugar (scant)	Grated rind 1 lemon
½ cup butter	Juice 2 lemons

Beat eggs until thick and lemon-colored. Continue beating and gradually add sugar. Then add grated rind of lemon juice and flour. Finally stir in slowly the melted butter. Fill uncooked pastry tarts with the mixture and cook in a moderate oven 15 or 20 min.

GRANDMOTHER HARRIS' BLUEBERRY POUND CAKE

2 sticks butter	3 cups sugar
1/2 cup Crisco	5 eggs
3 1/3 cups flour	1/2 tsp. baking powder
1/8 tsp. salt	1 cup evaporated milk
1 tbsp. vanilla extract	1 cup of frozen blueberries (drained)
or rum or lemon	3/4 cup powdered sugar
	3 tbsp. lemon juice

Grease and flour a tube pan. Preheat oven to 300 degrees.

Cream butter and Crisco. Add sugar and cream until light and fluffy. Sift dry ingredients together. Alternate addition of egg and flour mixture. Add milk and flavoring. Mix well. Fold in blueberries. Place a pan of water on the bottom rack and bake cake on the middle rack for about 1 hr. and 15 minutes. Let cake stand for 10 minutes before removing from pan.

While cake is cooling, mix powdered sugar with lemon juice to form a glaze for the cake. Pour over cake while it is still warm.

CAKES, PIES & COOKIES

LEMON ICE BOX CAKE

1 cup finely crushed chocolate
cookies crumbs (about 16 wafers)
6 tbsps. sugar
2 tbsps. butter, melted
2 eggs, separated

1 (15 oz.) can sweetened condensed
milk
1 tbsp. grated lemon rind
1/2 cup fresh lemon juice
1/4 tsp. almond extract

Combine crumbs, 2 teaspoons of sugar and butter. Press 1 cup of mixture on bottom and sides of buttered refrigerator tray; chill. Reserve remaining crumbs for top. Beat egg yolks until thick; add condensed milk. Add rind, juice, almond extract; stir until thick. Beat egg whites; gradually add remaining sugar and beat until stiff. Fold into condensed milk and lemon mixture. Pour into tray. Top with crumbs. Freeze until firm, 4-6 hours.

Orange Icing

2 cups confectioners sugar
3 tbsps. orange juice
Grated rind of 1 orange

Mix sugar, orange juice and rind together. Beat until smooth.

ORANGE CREAM CAKE

3 egg whites
1 cup sugar
3 egg yolks
1/2 cup milk
1 1/2 cups pastry flour

2 tsps. baking powder
1/4 tsp. salt
1/4 cup soft butter
1 tsp. vanilla

Beat egg whites to a froth, add 1/3 cup sugar and beat until mixture will stand in points. Beat yolks, add milk with 2/3 cup sugar. Beat in flour sifted with baking powder and salt. Add vanilla and softened butter (not melted). Beat well. Fold in egg whites. Turn into well greased and floured 8" layer pans. Bake 30 minutes in slow oven 325°F.

NUT CAKE

3 cups flour sifted
1 3/4 cups sugar
2 tsps. baking powder
1 1/2 tsps. salt

Sift above into bowl

1 cup nuts, chopped
1 cup shortening
3/4 cup milk
2 tsps. vanilla
2 eggs

Add to above in bowl

Beat s minutes at medium speed, add 2 more eggs. Beat 2 more minutes; fold in one cup chopped nuts. Put in oven 350 degrees about 45 minutes. Grease and dust tube with flour. Glaze–2 tsp. white corn syrup and 2 tsp. butter and boil 3 minutes. Decorate cake with cherries or other fruits, then put on glaze.

OLD FASHIONED APPLE CAKE

1/4 cup shortening
1/2 cup sugar
1 egg
Dash lemon juice
1 1/2 tsp. baking powder
Pinch salt
1/3 cup milk
1/2 tsp. vanilla
1 cup flour, sifted

Topping
2 apples, sliced thin
1 tbsp. butter
1/4 cup brown sugar
1 tsp. cinnamon

Put in greased round cake tin. Top with sliced apples placed close together and dot with butter and sprinkle with sugar and cinnamon. Bake in 350°F oven about 25 minutes. Serve with whipped cream.

ORANGE CAKE

2/3 cup shortening
1 1/2 cups sugar
3 eggs
3 cups flour
3 tsps. baking powder

1 tsp. salt
3/4 cup orange juice
1/4 cup water
Grated rind 1 orange

Cream shortening, sugar and egg yolks. Mix and sift flour, baking powder and salt and add alternately with combined orange juice, water and grated rind, to first mixture. Stir in beaten whites. Pour in 3 greased layer pans or 1 long pan and bake in 375°F oven 20 to 25 minutes for layers, 30 to 35 minutes for one pan. Cool. Spread orange filling between layers and orange icing on top.

CAKES, PIES & COOKIES

ROBERT E. LEE SPONGE CAKE

9 eggs, beaten separately until very light
1 lb. sugar
½ lb. flour

Pinch of salt
Lemon flavoring
Bake in layers

Filling

1 lb. sugar dissolved in juice of one lemon

3 oranges, squeeze and press to get flavor of the rind and all of the pulp
1 large cup grated coconut

Put between layers and on top so juice will seep through. Cover the cake when done with dry cocoanut.

LAFAYETTE FRENCH SILK

1 cup flour
1/2 cup pecans, chopped

1 cup brown sugar
1/4 cup butter, softened

Preheat oven to 400 degrees and mix all ingredients well. Spread on the bottom of a buttered 9x13 baking dish and bake for 15 minutes. Remove from oven, stir, and pat down smooth and put in the refrigerator.

topping:

1 cup butter, softened
1 1/2 cups sugar
2 tsps. vanilla

4 eggs
3 oz. unsweetened chocolate, melted

Cream butter and sugar. Add vanilla, chocolate and eggs, one at a time. Beat 5 minutes after each egg. Fill crust and chill several hours. Serve with whipped cream.

AMERICAN REVOLUTION PUDDING

3 cups blueberries
1 1/2 cups flour
1 cup brown sugar
2 tsp. baking powder
1 cup sugar
2 tsp. orange rind, grated
2 cups heavy cream

2 eggs
dash of vanilla
2/3 cup butter, softened
6 tbsp. butter
1/2 tsp. salt
3/4 cup orange juice
1/3 cup Grand Marnier

Preheat oven to 350 degrees. Simmer blueberries in brown sugar and the 6 tablespoons butter. Cream sugar, 2/3 cup butter and vanilla. Add eggs and continue beating. Sift flour, baking powder and salt into mixture. Add orange rind and juice. Place blueberry mixture in bottom of a 3 quart baking dish. Pour batter over berries. Bake for 45 minutes. Whip cream and add Grand Marnier. Serve as a topping for each serving. Yields 10 servings.

BANANA GINGER PIE   GINGERSNAP PIE SHELL

1 envelope unflavored gelatin
2/3 cup sugar
¾ cup water
1 tsp. grated lemon rind
3 tbsps. lemon juice
1 cup mashed bananas (2 medium)
2 unbeaten egg whites
1 Gingersnap Pie Shell

1 cup crushed gingersnaps
2 tbsps. melted butter

Mix gelatin and sugar together in the top of a double boiler. Add water. Place over boiling water and stir until gelatin is thoroughly dissolved. Remove from heat. Add lemon rind and juice and bananas. Chill until mixture mounds slightly when dropped from a spoon. Add egg whites and beat with a rotary beater until mixture begins to hold its shape. Turn into cooled pie shell and chill until firm. Makes 8 servings.

Blend together cookies and butter. Press firmly against bottom and sides of a 9" pie plate. Bake in moderate oven 375°F for 6 minutes. Cool.

CAKES, PIES & COOKIES

BUTTER FROSTING

1 cup confectioner's sugar
1 tsp. butter

2 tsps. milk
1/4 tsp. flavoring

Beat together and spread on cake.

CARAMEL FROSTING

1/4 cup butter
3/4 cup light brown sugar
1/4 cup evaporated milk

2 1/2 to 3 cups sifted confectioners' sugar
dash of salt

Melt butter in saucepan over medium heat and add brown sugar and milk. Heat until sugar dissolves. Cool slightly, then beat in confections' sugar, vanilla and salt. This will frost a 2-layer cake. Note: This frosting is good with the Jam Cake on page 19.

SEVEN-MINUTE FROSTING

2 egg whites
1/4 tsp. cream of tartar

1 1/2 cups sugar
1 teaspoon vanilla

Combine all ingredients except vanilla in 1/3 cup of water in the top of a double boiler. Beat until well blended, about one minute on high speed. Place over rapidly boiling water and beat continually for 5 minutes or until soft peaks are formed. Remove from water and add vanilla. Turn frosting into a bowl and continue beating for 2 to 3 minutes. This should frost a two-layer cake.

CRUSTY COCONUT PIE

1/2 cup milk	1 cup sugar
1 1/4 cup coconut (1 can)	3 eggs, slightly beaten
1/4 cup butter	1 tsp. vanilla or lemon extract

Pour milk over coconut and set aside while creaming butter and sugar. Add eggs and beat mixture well. Add milk, coconut and flavoring. Pour into unbaked pie shell. Bake at 350°F for 30 minutes.

DEEP DISH APPLE PIE

2 1/2 qts. sliced apples (9 to 12 apples)	1/4 tsp. salt
1 1/2 cups sugar	Dash of mace
1/2 tsp. cinnamon	3 tbsps. butter
1/2 tsp. nutmeg	

Pare and slice apples. Fill an oblong glass baking dish (about 12"x 8"x2") with apples. Mix dry ingredients and sprinkle over apples, mixing lightly. Dot with butter. Roll pie crust thin; place on top. Brush crust with cream—cut slits. Bake in hot oven (450°F) for 15 minutes. Then reduce heat to 350°F and cook 45 min. longer.

FAVORITE COCONUT CAKE

1 cup hot milk	2 1/2 cups flour, sifted
2 cups sugar	3 tsps. vanilla
6 egg	3 tsps. baking powder
1/2 cup butter	1/2 cup black walnuts, chopped

Preheat oven to 350 degrees. Grease and line three 9-inch cake pans with waxed paper. Separate eggs and reserve four whites for the icing. Beat egg yolks, 2 egg whites and sugar at medium-high speed until light and fluffy, at least 5 minutes. Melt butter in hot milk. Add 1/2 cup flour to eggs and sugar mixture. Add half of the hot milk mixture, 1 cup flour and remaining hot milk. Then add the rest of the flour, vanilla, baking powder and nuts. Pour into cake pans and bake 20 minutes. Cool slightly before removing from pans.

COCONUT FROSTING

1 1/2 cups sugar	1/2 tsp. cream of tartar
1/2 cup water	1 tsp. vanilla
4 egg whites	2 cups fresh coconut, shredded

Boil sugar and water for 2 minutes. Beat egg whites and cream of tartar until eggs stand up in stiff peaks, but are not dry. Pour boiling syrup into egg whites, beating at highest speed on mixer. When icing becomes stiff enough to spread, add vanilla. Spread between layers, on top and sides of cake. Sprinkle with coconut.

CAKES, PIES & COOKIES

GREEN TOMATO PIE

5 medium size green tomatoes	3 tbsps. butter
1 cup sugar	¼ tsp. salt
6 slices lemon (cut thin)	Allspice—nutmeg

Drop tomatoes in boiling water for a few minutes to loosen skin—take out and peel.

Line pie pan with your favorite pie dough. Sprinkle small amount of sugar on bottom of pie shell. Arrange sliced tomatoes in shell—a layer at a time. Cover with half the sugar—3 slices of lemon—good sprinkling of allspice and nutmeg. Dot with half the butter. Repeat this sequence until pie is filled. Cover with plain or latticed top and bake in a moderate (350°F) oven for 40 to 45 minutes.

SEVEN DAY PRUNE CAKE

3 eggs	1 1/2 cups prunes or raisins
1 1/2 cups sugar	3/4 cup shortening
2 3/4 cups flour	1/2 tsp. salt
1 tsp. cinnamon	1 1/2 tsp. soda
3/4 cup boiling coffee	

Preheat oven to 375 degrees. Grease and flour a loaf pan. Cook prunes for 10 min., drain and cool. Chop prune meat to a fine consistency. Cream sugar and shortening. Add eggs and prunes. Add flour, salt and spices plus 1/2 teaspoon soda. Add coffee with one teaspoon soda. Bake at 375 degrees for 25 minutes.

CHOCOLATE REESE CUPS

1 lb. confectioners' sugar	12 oz. chocolate chips
1 cup butter	2 tbsps. butter
1 cup peanut butter	1/2 block paraffin

Cream sugar, butter and peanut butter until well-blended. Shape into one inch diameter balls and chill. Melt chocolate chips, butter and paraffin. Dip the chilled balls with a toothpick in the chocolate mixture. Yields 50.

MAGIC PIE CRUST

1 cup shortening	2 tsps. baking powder
1/2 cup boiling water	3 cups pastry flour
1/2 tsp. salt	

Heat a mixing bowl by pouring boiling water into it. Let stand a minute or two, then pour water out.

Put shortening into this bowl and pour boiling water over it and beat with a fork until it is light and creamy. Sift dry ingredients together into the liquid. More flour will be needed to mold on board.

This dough is rather hard to get into shape, but it can be done, and is like a French pastry. This makes 2 good-sized pies.

MARLBOROUGH PIE

6 tart apples	1 lemon, juice and grated rind
1 tsp. butter	1 cup sugar
2 eggs, beaten	

Cook and strain the apples; add the butter and cool. Add the eggs, lemon rind, and sugar. Put in a deep dish pie shell and bake in a moderate oven 375°F for one hour or until the crust is done. Garnish with small cakes of puff paste baked separately, if desired. Makes one 9″ pie.

MOCK CHERRY PIE

1 cup cranberries (chopped fine)	1 tbsp. flour mixed with
1/2 cup raisins (chopped fine)	1 cup sugar

Pour over the mixture 1 cup boiling water. Add 1 tsp. vanilla. Cook until thickened. Bake with two crusts.

MT. VERNON LEMON CHESS PIE

1/2 lb. butter	1/2 tsp. salt
1 3/4 cups sugar	3 lemons, juice and grated rind
6 eggs	

Cream butter and sugar. Add one by one 6 whole eggs, 1/2 tsp. salt and the juice and grated rind of lemons. Pour into 2 unbaked pie shells. Cook at 400°F or 450°F until browned.

CAKES, PIES & COOKIES

ORANGE CHIFFON PIE

Crust

1/4 cup butter or margarine
1 cup marshmallow creme
1/2 cup finely shreaded coconut

1/4 tsp. vanilla
3 cups bite-size shredded rice, crushed
to 1 1/2 cups

Butter an 8″ or 9″ pie plate. Heat and stir butter and marshmallow creme over hot water until syrupy. Stir in vanilla, coconut, and cereal crumbs. Press into pie plate.

Filling

1 tbsp. unflavored gelatin
1/4 cup water
4 eggs separated
1 cup sugar, divided
2 tbsps. lemon juice

1/2 cup orange juice
1 tbsp. grated orange rind
1/2 tsp. salt
2 tbsps. toasted coconut (optional)

Soften gelatin in the water. Beat egg yolks and 1/2 cup sugar in top of double boiler. Add orange and lemon juice and salt. Blend thoroughly. Heat and stir over hot water until mixture coats a spoon, about 20 minutes. Put into pie crust and chill thoroughly before serving.

PINEAPPLE CHIFFON PIE

1 tbsp. gelatin
1/4 cup cold water
1 1/4 cups crushed pineapple
4 eggs

1/4 tsp. salt
1 tbsp. lemon juice
1/2 cup sugar

Soak gelatin in cold water about 5 minutes. Beat egg yolks slightly and add 1/4 cup sugar, pineapple, lemon juice and salt. Cook over boiling water until custard consistency. Add softened gelatin, stir thoroughly. Cool.

When mixture begins to thicken, fold in stiffly beaten egg whites to which have been added the other 1/4 cup sugar. Fill baked pie shell and chill.

Just before serving cover with a thin layer of whipped cream, flavored with pineapple juice and sugar.

PECAN PIE

3 eggs, slightly beaten	1/8 tsp. salt
1 cup sugar	1/2 to 1 cup of pecan pieces
1 cup light corn syrup	1 tsp. vanilla
Pinch of cinnamon	8 inch unbaked pie shell

Mix the ingredients, adding the nuts last. Pour into an 8 inch square shallow pan, lined with pastry, or into a pie plate of that size lined with pastry. Bake at 450°F for 10 minutes. Reduce the heat to 325°F and bake till filling is firm. Cooking time is about 50 minutes. When done, the top will be firm and crusty with the pecans showing.

PECAN PIE

6 eggs	2 tbsps. melted butter
1 1/2 cups corn syrup (dark)	Vanilla to taste
1/2 cup Vermont syrup	2 cups pecans
1 cup sugar	Pastry for 10" pie

Beat eggs and sugar together. Add vanilla to butter, then add to egg-sugar mixture. Add syrups and pour over pecans. Bake at 300°F for 45 minutes.

PECAN PIE

1/2 cup sugar	1/2 tsp. salt
1 cup dark corn syrup	3 eggs slightly beaten
1 cup pecan halves	Piece of butter
1 tsp. vanilla	

Mix well. Pour into *chilled* pastry shells. Bake 40 to 50 minutes 365°F.

SQUASH PIE

1 1/2 cups cooked, sieved squash	1/4 tsp. nutmeg
1 cup dark brown sugar	1 tsp. salt
1 tsp. cinnamon	1 cup milk
1 tsp. ginger	3 beaten eggs
1/2 tsp. clove	

Mix spices and salt with sugar and mix with the squash. Add milk, then beaten eggs. Pour into large, unbaked pie shell and bake 55 minutes at 350°F.

CAKES, PIES & COOKIES

PUMPKIN CHIFFON PIE

1 envelope plain gelatin
1/4 cup cold water
3 eggs
1 cup sugar

1 1/4 cups canned or cooked fresh
  pumpkin
2/3 cup milk
1/2 tsp. each of ginger, nutmeg,
  cinnamon and salt

Beat eggs yolks slightly, add 1/2 the cup of sugar, pumpkin, milk, and seasonings. Cook in double boiler until custard consistency, stirring constantly. Soften gelatin in cold water and dissolve in hot custard. Cool, and when mixture begins to thicken, fold in stiffly beaten egg whites, to which have been added the remaining 1/2 cup of sugar. Turn into a baked pie shell (a deep one) and place in refrigerator for a few hours. Top with light layer of flavored whipped cream. This is a delicious Fall and Winter dessert.

ALMOND MERINGUE COOKIES

1 1/4 cups soft margarine
2 cups sugar
1/2 tsp. vanilla
1/2 tsp. almond

2 eggs
4 cups sifted flour
1/2 tsp. salt

Cream butter and sugar and flavoring, add eggs one at a time. Beat until light and add flour. Shape into rolls and wrap in waxed paper and chill over night. Cut in 1/8 inch slices. Spread with topping and bake in 375°F oven 8 to 10 minutes.

TOPPING FOR COOKIES

3 egg whites
1/4 tsp. salt
1/2 cup sugar

1 tbsp. cinnamon
3/4 cup ground almonds

Beat egg whites and mix well. Spread on top of cookies before baking.

PUMPKIN PIE

1 can pumpkin	$\frac{1}{2}$ tsp. nutmeg
3 eggs	$\frac{1}{2}$ tsp. cinnamon
2 tbsps. flour	$\frac{1}{4}$ tsp. mace
2 tbsps. butter, melted	$\frac{1}{4}$ tsp. allspice
1 cup brown sugar, packed	$\frac{1}{2}$ tsp. salt
$\frac{1}{2}$ tsp. ginger	$1\frac{1}{4}$ cups thin cream or top milk

Beat eggs until thick. Add pumpkin. Add sugar, flour and butter. Add spices and then the milk. Pour into unbaked 9″ or 10″ pie shell. Bake at 425°F for 15 minutes, then 375°F for 30 to 40 minutes. Remove and cool.

Before serving beat ½ pint heavy cream until thick, add 1 tbsp. sherry, sugar to taste, and 2 tbsps. candied ginger cut fine. Spread over top of pie.

SWEET POTATO PIE

2 cups boiled mashed sweet potatoes	4 eggs
1 cup butter	2 cups sugar
1 lemon, juice and rind	$\frac{1}{2}$ tsp. mace
4 ozs. whiskey	

Cream sugar and butter. Add eggs and potatoes, whiskey and lemon juice. Put in baked shell. Cook in medium oven 375°F for 50 minutes. Sprinkle with powdered sugar. Makes 2 pies.

COOKIE JAR GINGERSNAPS

2 cups sifted flour	$\frac{3}{4}$ cup shortening
1 tsp. ginger	1 cup sugar
1 tsp. cinnamon	1 egg
2 tsps. baking soda	$\frac{1}{4}$ cup molasses
1 tsp. salt	Granulated sugar

Measure flour, ginger, soda, cinnamon and salt into sifter. Cream shortening until soft; gradually add sugar creaming after each addition until the mixture is fluffy. Beat in egg and molasses. Sift dry ingredients over creamed mixture and blend well. Form teaspoonfuls of dough into small balls by rolling them lightly, one at a time, between the palms of hands. Roll dough balls in granulated sugar to cover entire outside surface. Place 2″ apart on greased cookie sheet and bake at 350°F for 12 to 15 minutes. Makes 4 doz.

CAKES, PIES & COOKIES

BROWNIES

2 sqs. unsweetened chocolate
1/2 cup fat
1 cup sugar
2 eggs, slightly beaten
3/4 cup sifted flour

1/2 tsp. baking powder
1/2 tsp. salt
1 cup chopped nuts
1 tsp. vanilla

Melt chocolate and fat together over hot water. Cool slightly. Add sugar and the chocolate mixture to eggs and beat. Sift together the flour, baking powder and salt. Add to the first mixture. Stir in the nuts and vanilla. Pour in 9″ square greased pan. Bake at 350°F for 30 minutes.

DATE HERMITS

3 eggs
1 cup sugar
1 cup flour
1 tsp. baking powder
1/4 tsp. salt

1 tsp. vanilla
1 1/2 cups chopped dates
1 cup broken nut meats
1 cup powdered sugar

Beat eggs, add sugar; beat 1 min. Add flour, baking powder, salt, vanilla, dates and nuts. Pour into shallow pan and bake in moderate oven for 30 min. Remove, cut into 1 1/2 in. squares and roll in powdered sugar at once. Makes about 4 dozen hermits.

DATE SQUARES

Cook until thick 1 7-oz. pkg. dates, 3/4
  cup white sugar and 1 cup water.
Mix together:
1 3/4 cups rolled oats
1 cup brown sugar

1 1/2 cups flour
1 tsp. soda
3/4 cup melted butter or margarine

Spread 1/2 mixture on bottom of pan 7 1/2 x11. Pat down firmly. Spread date mixture over this and remainder of crumb mixture over top. Bake 25 min. in 375°F oven.

129

DATE SQUARES A LA MODE

1½ cups cut dates
¼ cup brown sugar, firmly packed
½ cup water
1 cup cornflake crumbs
1 cup sifted flour

½ tsp. baking soda
⅛ tsp. salt
¾ cup brown sugar, firmly packed
¾ cup margarine
1 qt. vanilla ice cream

To make filling combine dates, sugar and water in medium sized saucepan. Cook over low heat, stirring constantly, until a soft paste is formed. Remove from heat and cool.

Sift together flour, soda and salt; mix thoroughly with sugar. Cut in butter until mixture is crumbly. Stir in cornflake crumbs. Press half the crumb mixture into bottom of greased pan. Spread evenly with date filling. Top with remaining crumb mixture. Bake in slow oven, 325°F, until top is lightly brown. Cool, cut into squares and serve with vanilla ice cream on top.

EASY SUGAR COOKIES

2/3 cup salad oil
¾ cup sugar
2 cups flour
½ tsp. salt

1 tsp. baking powder
1 tsp. vanilla
1 tsp. almond flavor
2 eggs, well beaten

Mix, drop by teaspoon on baking sheet. Dip a small glass in salad oil, then into a shallow dish of sugar and press each cookie to a flat, perfect round. Bake in moderate oven. Remove from sheet while hot.

BUTTERSCOTCH COOKIES

2 cups brown sugar
2 eggs
1 tsp. vanilla
1½ cups nuts
4 cups flour

1 cup butter and lard mixed
1 level tsp. of cream of tartar
1 level tsp. soda
1½ cups dates
¼ tsp. salt

Sift flour and measure. Re-sift with soda, cream of tartar and salt. Cream fat and sugar until thoroughly blended. Add eggs beaten light & vanilla. Sift in part of dry ingredients. Then add nuts & dates which have been cut in pieces. Divide dough into four parts. Shape into rolls and let stand over night in a cool place, wrapped in waxed paper. Slice ¼ in. thick and bake in hot oven (400°F).

CAKES, PIES & COOKIES

GINGER SNAPS

3 lbs. flour
1 lb. butter
1 lb. sugar
1 pt. molasses

1 tsp. ginger
2 tsp. cinnamon
1/2 tsp. red pepper

Roll very thin, bake quickly. These are quite hot, but delicious.

COCONUT NUT SQUARES

Mix together in a square pan:

2 tbsps. confectioners sugar
1 cup cake flour
1/2 cup shortening

Bake for 30 minutes at 350°F. While this is baking, prepare the following:

1 1/4 cups brown sugar
1/2 cup coconut
2 eggs
1 1/2 tsps. baking powder

1/2 cup nut meats
2 tbsps. flour
1/4 tsp. salt

After the first mixture has baked for 30 minutes, spread this on top and bake for 30 minutes more at 350°F.

HERMITS

1 1/2 cups sugar
1 cup butter
3 eggs
3 cups flour
1 tsp. cinnamon

1 tsp. allspice
1 tsp. soda dissolved in
2 tsps. hot water
1 cup raisins

Drop in teaspoonfuls on greased sheet and bake in moderate oven.

Variations: Omit spices and raisins. Use 1/4 tsp. soda. Add any extract. Nuts of any kind make a rich cooky that keeps fresh indefinitely.

GINGERSNAPS

1 cup shortening	4 cups sifted flour
1/2 cup butter	4 tsp. baking soda
2 cups sugar	2 tsps. cloves
2 eggs	2 tsps. cinnamon
1/2 cup molasses	2 tsps. ginger

Work butter and fat together and gradually work in sugar until mixture is fluffy. Now beat in the eggs and molasses thoroughly. Sift dry ingredients and mix into creamed batter. Roll pieces of dough into 1 inch balls and roll in sugar. Place on cookie sheet (greased) about 3" apart. Bake at 350°F about 12 minutes.

ICE BOX COOKIES

1 cup shortening	1 tsp. salt
2 eggs, beaten	2 tsps. baking powder
3 1/2 cups flour	1 tsp. vanilla
2 cups brown sugar	

Blend crisco and sugar. Add eggs and sifted dry ingredients. Mix well and add flavoring. Shape into rolls about 3 inches in diameter and place in ice box to harden. Slice about 1/8 inch thick. Sprinkle with a mixture of

1/4 cup sugar
1/2 tsp. cinnamon
1/2 tsp. nutmeg

Bake in moderate oven 350°F for about 10 minutes.

LEMON PECAN OATMEAL COOKIES

1 cup flour	1 egg
1/2 tsp. salt	1 tbsp. grated lemon rind
1/2 tsp. soda	3 tbsps. lemon juice
1/2 cup shortening	1/2 cup chopped nuts
1/2 cup brown sugar	1 1/2 cups rolled oats
1/2 cup white sugar	

Sift together flour, soda, salt into bowl. Add shortening, sugars, egg, lemon rind and lemon juice. Beat until smooth. Fold in pecans and oats. Drop by teaspoonful onto greased cookie sheet. Bake 375°F 10 minutes. Yield 3 1/2 doz.

Walnuts can be used in place of pecans.

SALADS

SPRING SALAD WITH BASIL DRESSING

½ head lettuce
2 cups raw spinach
½ cup sliced radishes
1 cup sliced spring onions
2 cups diced fresh tomatoes
1¼ tsp. salt

¼ tsp. ground black pepper
½ tsp. crumbled whole basil leaves
¼ tsp. garlic powder
3 tbsp. fresh lemon juice
3 tbsp. olive or salad oil

Chill all vegetables. Tear lettuce and spinach into bite-size pieces and place in a salad bowl with other vegetables. Mix seasonings, lemon juice and oil; add. Toss lightly. Serve at once.

Serves 8.

HOT POTATO SALAD

3 cups diced raw potatoes
4 slices bacon
1/4 cup finely chopped onion
1 tbsp. flour
1 tsp. powdered dry mustard

1 tsp. salt
1 tbsp. sugar
1/2 cup water
1 egg, beaten
1/4 cup vinegar

Cook potatoes in a small amount of boiling salted water until tender. Drain.

Cook bacon in a fry pan until crisp. Remove from pan and chop. Using 2 tablespoons of the bacon fat, cook onions until golden brown. Blend flour, mustard, salt, and sugar into the fat. Stir in the water and boil for 2 minutes.

Add about 2 tablespoons of the hot mixture to the beaten egg, then stir this into the rest of the mixture. Add vinegar and reheat. Pour the hot dressing over the hot diced potatoes. Mix in the chopped bacon. Serve hot. 5 or 6 servings.

JELLIED CREAM SALAD

1 tsp. gelatin
1/4 cup cold water
1/2 cup boiling water
1 cup cream

1 cup mayonnaise
1 cup grated cheese
1/2 cup olives chopped
1/2 cup pecan meats chopped

Soak gelatin in cold water, dissolve in boiling water. Cool. Add cream whipped, mayonnaise and cheese. Salt, cayenne and paprika to taste. Place in refrigerator. When mixture begins to thicken, add olives and nuts. Place in molds and allow to harden. Serve on lettuce and garnish with mayonnaise.

JELLIED TOMATO-CREAM CHEESE SALAD

1 can tomato soup
2 cakes cream cheese
1 tsp. granulated gelatin
1 1/2 cups chopped celery

1 green pepper (chopped)
1 tsp. onion
1/4 cup water

Soak gelatin in cold water 5 min. Dissolve in boiling tomato soup. Cool slightly, add to cream cheese which has been rinsed in cold water and left damp.

SALADS

CEYLON ONION SAMBOL (SALAD)

1 large onion peeled
1 medium cucumber
1 medium green pepper, seeds
  removed

Juice of 1/2 lemon
1/2 tsp. salt
1/2 tsp. ground black pepper
3 hard-cooked eggs, peeled

Slice thin the onion, cucumber, and green pepper. Combine in bowl. Add lemon juice, salt and black pepper. Mix lightly. Cut eggs in half. Arrange on onion and cucumber mixture. Chill. Serve as an accompaniment to curry and rice.

FROZEN FRUIT SALAD

1 cup heavy cream whipped
1/2 cup Royal Anne cherries (halved
  and pitted)
1/2 cup Bing cherries
1/2 cup pears diced and drained
1/2 cup peaches, diced and drained

1/2 cup pineapple diced and drained
1/8 cup powdered sugar
1/2 cup pineapple juice
1/2 cup mayonnaise
1/4 tsp. lemon rind grated
1/2 cup marshmallows

Mix diced fruit and set aside—drain; mix pineapple juice, mayonnaise, lemon rind and sugar. Fold in whipped cream and fruit. Put in mold and freeze.

GOLDEN SALAD

1 tbsp. gelatine
1/4 cup cold water
1 cup pineapple juice
1 1/2 cups pineapple
1/4 cup sugar

1 medium carrot grated
1/4 cup vinegar
1/2 cup orange juice
1 cup oranges cut up
1 tsp. mayonnaise

Soak gelatine in cold water 5 minutes. Dissolve in hot pineapple juice, add sugar, salt, orange juice and vinegar. When jelly begins to stiffen add other ingredients. Turn into mold. When nearly firm put in 1 teaspoon mayonnaise. When this is firm, fill mold with salad.

BING CHERRY SALAD

1 can Blackbing cherries
1 pkg. cherry jello
1 cup cherry juice

1 cup Port wine
Almonds
1½ tbsps. gelatine

Heat juice and melt jello in it, add nuts and whole fruit. Add 1½ tablespoons gelatine.

HEAVENLY FROZEN SALAD

4 egg yolks
4 tbsps. tarragon vinegar
4 tbsps. sugar
1 pt. heavy cream

1 can sliced pineapple
½ lb. marshmallows
¼ lb. shelled pecans

To the egg yolks add vinegar and sugar. Cook these in a double boiler until stiff. Cool and then add heavy cream which has been whipped stiff. Next add sliced pineapple cut into small bits, marshmallows cut into quarters and pecans broken into small pieces. Freeze in refrigerator tray for 4 or 5 hours. Cover with wax paper to prevent icing. Serve this sliced on lettuce with mayonnaise to which has been added an equal part of whipped cream. This serves 12.

SEA DREAM SALAD

1 pkg. lime jello
1 cup grated cucumber, peeling and
   all
1 tsp. grated onion

½ tsp. salt
Dash cayenne pepper
1 cup boiling water
1 tbsp. vinegar

Grate cucumber, add onion, salt, pepper, then vinegar. Pour boiling water on lime jello. Stir till dissolved. Mix all well. Put in molds. Congeal. Finely chopped celery may be added.

RAW CRANBERRY SALAD

2 cups raw cranberries
2 oranges, grated rind of one
2 apples (or celery)

2 pkgs. lemon jello
3 cups of boiling water

Grind fruit, cover with sugar and let stand overnight. Add boiling water to jello and when cool add fruit mixture and pour in mold. Nuts can be added for variety.

SALADS

TOMATO MOUSSE SALAD

2 pkgs. of lemon jello
1 cup of tomato juice
1/2 cup of mayonnaise

1/4 cup of tomato ketchup
Dash of onion salt
1 pkg. of cream cheese

Melt on stove lemon jello in tomato juice but do not boil. Take off stove, and add mayonnaise, ketchup, and cream cheese and onion salt. Beat with electric mixer until smooth. Mold in ring or individual cups coated with mayonnaise. Keep in refrigerator until time to garnish and serve. Serve with French dressing.

COMMERCIAL MAYONNAISE

4 tsps. flour
3 tsps. oil
3/4 cup hot water
1/2 tsp. paprika
1/4 tsp. mustard

1/4 tsp. pepper
2 egg yolks or 1 whole egg (beaten)
3 tsps. acid (vinegar)
2 cups oil

Cook flour, 3 tsp. oil and hot water for 5 minutes stirring constantly. Add paprika, mustard, pepper, and egg yolks. Add oil and acid alternately.

CREAM DRESSING FOR LETTUCE

1 pt. sweet cream
2 tbsps. vinegar
2 tbsps. lemon juice
2 tbsps. sugar or more to taste

1/2 tsp. mustard
2 hard-boiled eggs
1/4 tsp. red pepper or more to taste
1/4 tsp. paprika

Mix yolks of eggs with red pepper, paprika, and mustard. Chop fine whites of eggs. Pour lemon juice and vinegar slowly into cream. Add sugar. Add mixture of yolks, red pepper and paprika. Add chopped whites of eggs. This makes a quart of dressing and will last for quite a while if kept in the ice-box. Used over garden leaf lettuce, it is delicious.

POTATO SALAD

1 pt. diced boiled potato
1 pt. diced raw celery
1/2 pt. chopped hard-boiled egg
1/2 cup chopped sweet pickle

1/2 cup minced parsley and onion
Salt and paprika to taste
1 cup mayonnaise

Mix to desired consistency and serve on lettuce leaf with slice of tomato or cold beet. Two quarts serves twelve people.

POTATO-CHEESE SALAD

2 cups diced cooked potatoes
2 hard-cooked eggs, coarsely
   chopped
1 tsp. salt
1/2 cup celery, coarsely chopped

2 tbsps. chopped onion
1 1/2 cups diced cheese
1/2 cup mayonnaise
1/4 cup sweet pickle juice

Thin mayonnaise with pickle juice. Combine with remaining ingredients.

Chill salad thoroughly to blend flavor.

Serve on crisp salad greens. If desired garnish with sliced pickle. 4 Servings.

POTATO SALAD

4 medium-sized potatoes
3/4 cup hot cooked salad dressing
1 to 2 tbsps. finely chopped scallions
   or onions
1 tsp. salt

2 tbsps. chopped green pepper
1/2 cup finely cut celery
1/4 cup diced cucumber
2 hard-cooked eggs, chopped

Cook potatoes whole in the skins, peel and dice. Or pare, dice and cook them in a small amount of boiling salted water until tender. Drain.

Pour hot dressing over hot potatoes. Add scallions or onion and salt and mix carefully. Let cool for 10 to 15 minutes.

Mix in the rest of the ingredients.

Chill for 3 or 4 hours before serving. Makes about 1 quart.

SALADS

POTATO SALAD-SALMON PLATE

3 cups potato salad
Lettuce
1-lb. can chilled salmon
2 tomatoes, sliced

$\frac{1}{2}$ cucumber, sliced
4 lemon wedges
Parsley

Mold potato salad into four mounds. Place each on a lettuce leaf in center of platter.

Drain salmon and break into large chunks. Surround potato salad with salmon and with tomato and cucumber slices. Decorate with lemon wedges and parsley.

4 servings.

ROQUEFORT DRESSING

$\frac{1}{2}$ pt. sour cream
$\frac{1}{2}$ lb. Roquefort cheese or bleu cheese
1 tsp. sugar

$\frac{1}{2}$ tsp. salt
3 tbsps. cream or milk
1 tsp. mayonnaise

Pour sour cream in mixing bowl, add all ingredients except cheese. Mix well. Crumble cheese and add to mixture. Refrigerate about an hour then let stand at room temperature for 30 minutes before serving. Additional milk or cream may be added if a thinner dressing is desired.

SOUR CREAM SALAD DRESSING

2 hard boiled eggs
$\frac{1}{2}$ tsp. salt
$\frac{1}{2}$ tsp. dry mustard
$\frac{1}{4}$ pt. sour cream

4 tsps. vinegar
Pinch of sugar
Dash of red pepper

Mash yolks of eggs, add salt, mustard, sugar and red pepper. Blend in ¼ Pint of sour cream and vinegar. Stir in finely chopped whites of eggs and diced onion.

COLE SLAW DRESSING

¾ cup sugar
1 egg well beaten
1 tbsp. butter

1 tsp. flour
1 tsp. salt
1 dry or 2 tsps. mixed mustard

Beat well together. Add ½ cup water first, then ½ cup vinegar. Cook until thick. Pour hot over the chopped cabbage.

DASHER'S SALAD DRESSING

2 tbsps. mayonnaise
6 drops Tabasco
10 drops Worcestershire sauce

1 tbsp. Bar-B-Cue sauce
sauce
1½ tbsps. catsup

Mix above ingredients and serve on salads or use as cocktail dip.

FRENCH DRESSING FOR FRUIT SALAD

1 cup oil
¼ cup vinegar
½ cup powdered sugar
1 tsp. Worcestershire Sauce
1 tsp. salt (generous)

1 tsp. mustard
1 tsp. paprika
1 grated clove
Juice of 1 lemon
Juice of 1 orange

Mix all ingredients thoroughly and serve fruit salad on crisp lettuce.

FRUIT SALAD DRESSING

1 can pineapple juice
Juice of a small lemon
½ cup sugar
1 heaping tsp. flour

Small piece of butter
2 beaten eggs
Salt

Cook all in double boiler until thick. When ready to serve, add 1 jar of whipped cream.

HOT SAUCE FOR AVOCADOS

4 tbsps. melted butter
2 tbsps. tomato ketchup
2 tbsps. vinegar
½ tsp. salt

3 tsps. sugar
2 tsps. Worcestershire sauce
Dash of Tabasco

Put on stove and heat. Serve in halves of avocados. Do not peel. Garnish with shredded lettuce around avocado half.

PRESERVES & PICKLES

BREAD AND BUTTER PICKLES

25 to 30 medium size cucumbers
8 large white onions
2 large sweet peppers
½ cup salt
5 cups cider vinegar

5 cups sugar
2 tbsp. mustard seed
1 tsp. tumeric
½ tsp. ground cloves

Wash Cucumbers, slice thin as possible. Chop or grind through meat grinder onions and peppers. Combine with cucumbers, add salt and let stand 3 hours. Then drain. Combine vinegar, sugar and spices in large preserving kettle. Bring to boil, add the drained cucumbers, heat thoroughly but do not boil. Pack while hot in sterilized jars and seal.

ARTICHOKE OIL PICKLE

1 pkg. artichokes (8 qts.)	1 lb. white mustard seed
1/2 lb. ground mustard	1/2 oz. tumeric
1 qt. bottle sweet oil	1/2 lb. grated horseradish
Four blades mace	1/2 onion chopped fine
1 tsp. ground mustard	1 qt. vinegar (enough to thin down
4 tsps. brown sugar	ingredients)

Peel and cut artichokes in pieces one-half inch thick. Drop the oil in all seasoning as you do in mayonnaise (this is important), thin gradually with vinegar.

Keep artichokes in salt and water two or three days then draw and dry thoroughly. Put in a 2-gallon jar, pour over the above mixture and set in a vessel of water which must be kept boiling; boil 3 to 4 hours, but do not let them become soft, stir occasionally, and after taking off, stir constantly until cool.

BREAD AND BUTTER PICKLES

4 qts. cucumbers	1/2 cup salt
2 green peppers	1/2 tsp. ground cloves
1 qt. small white onions	2 tsps. mustard seed
5 cups Brown sugar	1 tsp. celery seed
1 1/2 tsps. tumeric	5 cups vinegar

Wash cucumbers and slice thin. Peel and slice onions. Seed and shred peppers. Mix all with salt and leave for 3 hours. Drain and rinse well with cold water. Add to syrup made with the brown sugar, tumeric, ground cloves, mustard seed, celery seed and vinegar. Fill jars and seal.

BREAD AND BUTTER PICKLES

3 qts. sliced cukes	1/2 tsp. ginger
3 onions	2 tbsps. mustard seed
1/2 cup salt	1 tsp. tumeric
1 cup vinegar	1/2 tbsp. celery seed
1 cup water	1 pod hot red pepper
3 cups brown sugar	1 piece horseradish
1 tsp. cinnamon	

Mix cukes, onions (sliced), let stand 5 hrs. Drain. Boil vinegar, water, sugar and seasonings 3 minutes. Add cukes and onion and simmer 10-20 minutes (do not boil). Pack into hot Ball jars and seal at once.

PRESERVES & PICKLES

BUSY DAY PICKLES

4 qts. peeled sliced (thick) cucumbers	5 cups sugar
8 small white onions	1½ tsps. tumeric
1 green pepper	½ tsp. ground cloves
1 sweet red pepper	2 tbsps. mustard seed
½ cup coarse medium salt	2 tbsps. celery seed
Ice cubes	5 cups vinegar

Slice cukes as desired. Add onions, peppers sliced or in strips. Add salt and cover with cracked ice and cukes. Let stand 3 hrs. Drain. Combine remaining ingredients. Pour over cucumber mixture. Bring to boil only. Seal in sterilized jars. Makes 8 pints. This improves in flavor as stored.

CABBAGE PICKLE

3 large cabbages	2 tbsps. white mustard seed
1 qt. of white onions	2 tbsps. celery seed
1½ qts. vinegar	2 tbsps. dry mustard
1 cup white sugar	2 tbsps. tumeric

Cut cabbage and onions and let stand overnight in salt brine. Do not cut cabbage too small. Next morning drain and freshen in cold water. Drain well before adding to vinegar. Let all come to a boil and cook for a few minutes. Season to taste. It may need more salt and vinegar, as it must be covered.

COUSIN HATTIE'S MANGO CHUTNEY

1 qt. apple vinegar	1½ cups chopped onions
7 cups brown sugar	3 tbsps. salt
2 pkgs. of seedless raisins	1½ tbsp. red pepper
10 cloves of garlic chopped fine	¾ cup root ginger crushed fine

Cook these ingredients in a kettle slowly for 40 minutes. Then put in 10 cups of mangoes which have been cut and peeled. Cook till thick. Peaches may substitute for mangoes.

CHOPPED ARTICHOKE PICKLE

3 qts. artichokes (slice after measuring)	1 qt. onions (chop after measuring)
	6 large green peppers (chop)
3 lbs. cabbage (chop after weighing)	

Pour over this 1 gallon water to which 1½ cups salt have been dissolved.

Let stand overnight.

Boil ½ gallon vinegar and 2 lbs. sugar for 5 minutes.

Add: 1 rounded tablespoon tumeric; 1 rounded tablespoon black pepper; 3 rounded tablespoons mustard seed; 1 rounded tablespoon celery seed.

Add ¾ cup flour which has been mixed with 9 ozs. French's prepared mustard and some of the vinegar. Let boil 5 to 10 minutes. Seal in sterilized jars. Yield: 11 pints.

CHUTNEY

2 ozs. garlic	3 lbs. seeded raisins
8 lbs. hard apples	1 lb. crystalized ginger
6 lbs. sugar	Salt to taste
2 lbs. onions	vinegar

Core and cut apples in small pieces. Put garlic and onion through meat grinder; take enough vinegar to boil these in; add sugar and boil ten minutes; add raisins and small amount of mustard; boil twenty minutes; add cut up ginger and, if desired, watermelon pickle and ground ginger to taste; cook a few minutes. Seal in sterilized jars.

COLD RELISH

4 carrots	2 pts. vinegar
2 large heads cabbage	2 pts. sugar
9 red peppers	2 tbsps. celery seed
9 green peppers	2 tbsps. mustard seed
8 medium sized onions	Dash red pepper
½ cup salt	

Put vegetables through the food chopper, then add salt and mix thoroughly. Add the rest of the ingredients, mix thoroughly, and seal in jars. Do not cook.

PRESERVES & PICKLES

CRANBERRY RELISH

1 lb. fresh cranberries
2 oranges

2 apples
2 cups sugar

Grind cranberries, oranges and apples together, including the skin of oranges and apples. Add sugar and let stand for a few hours or overnight before using. Delicious with chicken or pork.

GREEN TOMATO JOY

1 gal. green tomatoes
6 large onions
2 stalks celery
3 sweet red peppers
1 qt. vinegar
2 qts. sugar

1 tbsp. whole cloves
1 tbsp. allspice
1 tbsp. whole mustard seed
1 tsp. whole celery seed
2 tsps. salt
1/4 tsp. pepper

Slice tomatoes and onions. Cut celery and peppers in small pieces. Combine the remaining ingredients, put in large preserving kettle and bring to a boil. Add the tomato mixture and cook until tender. Pour into jars and seal while hot.

ICICLE PICKLES

Large cucumbers
3 cups white vinegar
1 cup water

3 cups sugar
1/4 cup salt

Peel cukes, remove seeds, cut in strips 1/2 in. wide. Cover with ice water and let stand overnight. Drain. Pack upright in sterilized jars. Boil vinegar, water, sugar for 3 minutes. Add salt and pour over cukes and seal. Let stand 6 weeks before using. Serve chilled as relish or hors d'oeuvres. Slices of dill or any other spices, onion or garlic may be put on top or bottom of cans if desired.

DILL TOMATO PICKLE

1 bud garlic	2 qts. water
1 stalk celery	1 qt. vinegar
1 green pepper quartered	1 cup salt
Make brine of water, vinegar and salt with a little dill to taste	

Boil and pour hot brine over the pickles in the jars and seal at once. These will be ready to use in 4 to 6 weeks.

EMERGENCY PICKLES

1 pt. sliced carrots	1 cup tender green beans
1 green pepper	3 cups sugar
1 or 2 sweet red peppers	1 cup vinegar
3 medium sized onions, sliced	1½ tsps. salt
1 tsp. tumeric	½ tsp. ground mustard

Chop peppers. Combine all ingredients and cook slowly until vegetables are tender but not soft. Pack into hot jars and seal at once.

ENGLISH CHOPPED PICKLE

1½ large white cabbage	½ gal. green tomatoes
½ gal. cucumbers, out of brine	15 large onions

Sprinkle with salt, let stand overnight, wash and drain. Add:

3 qts. vinegar	4 tbsps. celery seed
4 lbs. brown sugar	6 tbsps. white mustard seed
1 lb. raisins	1½ tsps. allspice
3 green peppers	1 tsp. ginger
3 red peppers	

Boil for 10 minutes. Put in jars.

FRUIT MARMALADE

3 oranges	1 No. 2 can Crushed Pineapple
1 lemon	1 small bottle Marachino Cherries (cut
6 cups sugar	in pieces)
½ cup water	

Put oranges and lemon through meat chopper. Mix all together; bring to a boil; simmer ¾ hours. Pour into sterilized glasses and cover with paraffin. Makes about 10 6 oz. glasses.

PRESERVES & PICKLES

EUCHRE CHERRIES

4 qts. stoned cherries
1 qt. vinegar
Sugar

Cover cherries with vinegar & let stand 24 hours, stirring frequently. Drain off vinegar, then mix one cup of sugar and one of cherries until all are used. Stand 24 hours again and stir as before, then put in jars and seal.

RIPE CUCUMBER PICKLES

Peel 5 large cucumbers, cut out seeds and cut into squares ½″ thick. Cover with hot water. Cook until can be pierced with fork. Add ½ tsp. alum.

Make syrup: 3½ lbs. white sugar   ½ tsp. oil of cloves
      1 pt. vinegar   ½ tsp. oil of cinnamon

Drain water off pickles. Pour hot syrup over pickles. Let stand overnight.

Drain off syrup and reheat. Pour syrup over pickles and seal into jars or put in covered crock.

GREEN TOMATO MINCE MEAT

1 peck green tomatoes   1 cup vinegar
5 lbs. sugar   2 tbsps. cloves
2 lbs. raisins   2 tbsps. cinnamon
1 tbsp. salt   1 oz. nutmeg
1 cup ground suet

Grind tomatoes, draw off juice, add as much cold water as there is juice, and scald. Repeat, and pour off water again.

Add sugar, raisins, salt, suet and vinegar. Boil 20 minutes, and add spices. Seal while hot. Makes 6 quarts.

ORANGE MARMALADE

2 oranges	11 glasses of water
2 lemons	4 lbs. of sugar

Chop the fruit fine, pour water over it, and let stand till next day. Cook very slowly for 1½ hours, then add sugar and cook slowly till it jells. Makes 12 glasses of marmalade.

PEACH CONSERVE

6 lbs. diced ripe peaches	2 tbsps. peach pits chopped
6 lbs. granulated sugar	1 small bottle maraschino cherries
3 oranges—pulp (grated rind of 1)	chopped
1 lemon—pulp	

Combine all ingredients except cherries and cook slowly 45 minutes. Then add cherries and continue cooking 15 minutes longer. Pour into small containers and seal.

PEAR AND PINEAPPLE HONEY

6 lbs. pears, ground in food chopper
5 lbs. sugar
1 can crushed pineapple

Weigh the fruit after it is ground, add the sugar and let stand over night. Cook slowly 2 or 3 hours. After it has been cooking 1 hour add the pineapple and continue cooking.

Place in sterilized glasses and seal.

PEPPER RELISH

1½ doz. red peppers	1½ qts. vinegar
1½ doz. green peppers	5 cups sugar
1½ doz. onions	¼ tsp. red pepper
1 cup salt	

Put peppers and onions through coarse meat grinder. Sprinkle with salt, allow to stand 15 minutes, drain and scald 3 times. Place vinegar on stove, add sugar, then peppers, onions and red pepper. Cook 30 minutes after it comes to a boil. Seal in jars while hot.

PRESERVES & PICKLES

MIXED PICKLE

1 qt. string beans
1 qt. green tomatoes
1 qt. celery
2 qts. green lima beans
8 ears corn
8 onions
6 red peppers

2 doz. small sweet pickles
1 qt. vinegar
6 cups sugar
1 cup flour
1/4 of a 1/4 pound box dry mustard
1 tbsp. tumeric

Cook corn, lima & string beans as you would for the table, salt to taste. Cut up tomatoes, celery, peppers & pickles. Put vinegar and sugar in enameled kettle on stove, add green vegetables and mix well. Add cooked vegetables and let come to a boil. Mix flour mustard & tumeric, add to above mixture and let boil again. Put in jars and seal tightly.

ORANGE JELLY

1 envelope gelatine
2 cups orange juice
1 cup orange segments

3 tbsps. sugar
1 pinch salt

Place orange juice, sugar, salt and gelatin in a saucepan over moderate heat and stir until gelatin is dissolved. Chill and when slightly thick, stir in orange segments.

PEPPER RELISH

12 red sweet peppers
12 green sweet peppers
3 hot red peppers
12 onions
2 cups cider vinegar

2 cups sugar
3 tbsps. salt
1 tbsp. mustard seed
1 tbsp. celery seed

Remove seeds. Peel onions. Grind. Cover with boiling water. Let stand 10 minutes. Drain thoroughly. Boil vinegar and spices. Add vegetables. Boil 10 minutes. Fill sterilized jars and seal.

PICKLED PEACHES

8 lbs. peaches
4 lbs. sugar
1 pint vinegar

Peel peaches, cover with sugar and let stand all night. In morning pour off juice and cook until thick. Add vinegar then put in peaches. Cook peaches until clear.

QUINCE HONEY

3 large unpared quinces
3 lbs. sugar
1 pt. water

Grate quinces, add sugar and water and boil 20 minutes, or until golden in color. Pour into glasses & seal while hot.

SWEET PICKLED PEACHES

7 lbs. fruit
3¾ lbs. sugar
1 qt. vinegar

2 ozs. whole cloves
2 ozs. stick cinnamon

Put the sugar into the preserving kettle with the vinegar and spices. Boil them for 5 min. after the sugar is dissolved. Pare the peaches and stick a clove into each one. Place a few at a time in the boiling syrup and cook them until they look clear, but are not softened enough to fall apart. When all are cooked, continue to boil the syrup until it is reduced nearly one half, and pour it over the peaches. Seal in jars.

SWEET PICKLES

½ bushel gherkins
1 gal. vinegar
1 cup granulated sugar
1 tsp. saccharine

1 cup salt
¾ cup dry mustard
Mixed spices
Celery seed

Mix sugar, saccharine & mustard and add to vinegar. Boil all together. Pack gherkins in pan. Sprinkle with salt, cover with boiling water and let stand overnight. Drain and pack in jars. Fill each jar with boiling vinegar mixture, add one teaspoonful of mixed spices and a pinch of celery seed to each jar and seal.

151

Publisher
BICAST PUBLISHING CO.
P.O. Box 2676
Williamsburg, Virginia 23187

Send me .... copies of "from Williamsburg Kitchens" @ $8.95 each, plus $1.00 for postage and handling. Virginia residents add 4 1/2% sales tax.

Enclosed is $ ....

NAME ....

ADDRESS ....

CITY .... STATE .... ZIP ....

Publisher
BICAST PUBLISHING CO.
P.O. Box 2676
Williamsburg, Virginia 23187

Send me .... copies of "from Williamsburg Kitchens" @ $8.95 each, plus $1.00 for postage and handling. Virginia residents add 4 1/2% sales tax.

Enclosed is $ ....

NAME ....

ADDRESS ....

CITY .... STATE .... ZIP ....